Judy Chicago

EDITED BY ELIZABETH A. SACKLER

LUCY LIPPARD
EDWARD LUCIE-SMITH
VIKI D. THOMPSON WYLDER

PHOTOGRAPHY BY DONALD WOODMAN

WATSON-GUPTILL PUBLICATIONS/NEW YORK

In honor of my mother, Else Sackler (1913–2000),
and my father, Arthur M. Sackler, M.D. (1913–1987).

Acknowledgments

Wilhelmina Cole Holliday, Susan Fisher Sterling, Arnold Lehman, Marc Mayer, John Bullard,
Lucy Lippard, Edward Lucie-Smith, Viki D. Thompson Wylder, Martha Conners, Stephanie
Morillo, Janet Bajan, Janet McKay, Carol Master, Neal Gantcher, Harriet Pierce, Alison Hagge, and
my dearest friend, colleague, and partner in crime, Barry Rosen.

—Elizabeth A. Sackler

Viki D. Thompson Wylder's essay is adapted from a piece that was originally published in
Trials and Tributes (Tallahassee, FL: Florida State University, 1999). The author thanks Florida
State University Museum of Fine Arts for their kind permission.

Senior Acquisitions Editor: Candace Raney
Senior Editor: Alison Hagge
Production Manager: Ellen Greene
Cover and interior design: Eric Baker Design Associates

The principal typefaces used in the composition of this book were 10-point Berthold Bodoni and
18-point Interstate.

First published in 2002 by Watson-Guptill Publications
a division of VNU Business Media, Inc.
770 Broadway, New York, NY 10003
www.watsonguptill.com

Library of Congress Cataloging-in-Publication Data

Lippard, Lucy R.
    Judy Chicago / Lucy R. Lippard, Edward Lucie-Smith, Viki D. Thompson Wylder ;
edited by Elizabeth A. Sackler.
                    p. cm.
Catalog of an exhibition in Washington, D.C. at the National Museum of
Women in the Arts.
Includes bibliographical references and index.
    ISBN 0-8230-2587-X
  1. Chicago, Judy, 1939---Exhibitions. 2. Feminism and art--Exhibitions.
I. Lucie-Smith, Edward. II. Thompson, Viki D. III. Sackler, Elizabeth A.
IV. National Museum of Women in the Arts (U.S.) V. Title.
    N6537.C48 A4 2002
    700'.92--dc21
                        2002003740

Manufactured in China
First printing, 2002
1 2 3 4 5 6 7 8 9 / 09 08 07 06 05 04 03 02

TABLE OF CONTENTS

FOREWORD

I met Judy Chicago for the first time in 1988 at her studio and home in Santa Fe, where she was living with her husband, Donald Woodman, and her beloved cats—Mully, Poppy, a new kitten Veronica, and the adored Sebastian.

Judy was entrenched in the creation of the *Holocaust Project*, tackling studies for *Treblinka/Genocide*. I was doing a site visit as the reviewer for her grant application to the Threshold Foundation.

The sequence of my visit is foggy. Did we go to the studio first, did we have tea and talk first, at what point was I introduced to Donald, the cats, the office? What remains vivid was Judy's vitality and brilliance, her profound desire to share the experience and process of her creativity.

I remember walking through Judy's studio, discussing images and the fusion of painting and photography for the project's final images. I remember sitting at her round table next to the kitchen, looking through the wall of windows at a large weeping willow (unusual for the dry Santa Fe foliage), and talking. Because she is a speaker, writer, instructor, and a vocal advocate for women in the arts, it is not surprising that Judy had excellent communication skills at her fingertips that she could call upon and implement at our meeting. What she could not have been aware of was my recognition of her genius. Having grown up with a genius father and opportunities to meet his peers in different fields, I recognized instantly her genius energy: enthusiasm, passion, quickness of mind, persistence, and a shining, almost innocent, intensity. For Judy, there is no such thing as "no" and all is possible.

I queried Judy: Why Feminist Art? Judy is a mother of contemporary Feminist Art, and in the beginning I could not understand why her art could not simply be art. Judy's earlier "prefeminist" works are brilliant. Why the delineation?

Judy's male professors found her elegantly symbolic work in the early 1960s distasteful, which ignited her activist soul. She responded by beginning the Feminist Art Program at California State University at Fresno. She created performance and environmental works. It was then that Feminist Art began and, in Edward Lucie-Smith's words, many of the "in your face" works took root. As an artist, Judy was enticed by any media that served her end. In 1964 she began spray painting. According to sculptor John Chamberlain, there was only one place to learn to spray paint—at auto body school. Judy alternately describes her apprenticeship (as the only woman—with 250 guys) as humiliating, exhilarating, hilarious. Judy's series of outstanding sprayed acrylic paintings eventually culminated in her last early feminist work, the masterpiece *Through the Flower*.

In 1974 Judy began *The Dinner Party*. The use of ceramics, china painting, embroidery, and weaving were a means and an end. Because these media were disdainfully described as inferior women's crafts by the male-dominated art world, one of Judy's goals was to tumble this artificial hierarchy by integrating her artistic esthetic and skill with those crafts, rendering them unequivocal equals of any work of "fine art." Judy began *The Dinner Party* alone, but eventually realized she needed a team. More than four hundred women collaborated with Judy until its completion in 1979. Since then *The Dinner Party* has been seen by more than one million people. Judy Chicago's *The Dinner Party* is recognized as an iconic work of fine art. It is also a monument to women, by women, using women's crafts.

Although Judy describes *The Dinner Party* as a symbolic history of women, in addition I believe *The Dinner Party* is a beacon and for some even a call to arms. I have repeatedly heard it described as sacred, even transcendent. There is no other work of art that has been as significantly powerful to as many women as *The Dinner Party*. There is no other work of art that opens the door to as endless an exploration of the contribution of women of the distant and not-so-distant past, inviting an abundance of education and inspiration.

This book, *Judy Chicago*, spans a unique and prolific career and therefore includes many early works that have never before been published. The exhibition, *Judy Chicago*—to be launched at the National Museum for Women in the Arts, Washington, D.C., in

October 2002—is an opportunity to see the breadth and range of Judy Chicago's oeuvre, her groundbreaking contributions to the world of art, to culture, and to women past, present, and future. She has fought the status quo with the same single-minded tenacity, resilience, and gumption with which she has conducted her life and forged her life's work.

This has been one of the most exciting relationships of my life. To share goals and visions, joke, laugh, argue with shrill voice, to collaborate with sober thoughtfulness, and to turn the world on its ear, is what it is to know and work with Judy Chicago, the woman, the artist. As with most important relationships, ours has had its highs and lows, but our shared goals, my patronage of her work, and our emotional similarities have brought us to this particularly pivotal moment in time. It has been an honor and a joy to guide *The Dinner Party* back to the Brooklyn Museum of Art for a five-month exhibition opening September 19, 2002, and to secure its permanent housing there in its own gallery.

It is with admiration and love for Judy, her genius, and the gifts she so generously shares with the world, that I give of my time and resources in hopes that others may also enjoy and reap from the extraordinary work of this great artist and founder of Feminist Art.

Elizabeth A. Sackler
New York City
18 March 2002

Childhood Fingerpainting, 1943 (AGE 4)

JUDY CHICAGO

>>> A MORAL VISION

Judy Chicago is a pivotal American artist for several reasons. One of the most obvious of these is that she is the author of one of the very few absolutely iconic works in the history of American art, *The Dinner Party*. No history of art in America, or indeed of twentieth-century art in general, can be thought of as being complete without some mention of it. Another reason is the fact that she has probably altered the lives of many people who have come into contact with what she does. The Feminist Movement in America is rich in important texts, but, despite the great quantity of Feminist Art that has been produced in the United States since the late 1970s, it has been substantially less successful in producing visual images that have entered the mainstream of American culture. Why then has Chicago been thought of as a controversial artist, when she is enormously central to the story of art in twentieth-century America?

To understand these paradoxes, one must try to step back a little. It is useful, for example, to ask if Chicago's work has relationships with other traditions in addition to the purely feminist one. As soon as the question is put, one sees that there are in fact a variety of interesting answers. If one looks at the whole history of American culture, interpreting this in its broadest sense, one immediately sees that it has been shaped by factors peculiar to itself. America did not evolve into a democracy, as the nations of Europe did; it began with democratic ideals from the very beginning. American writers have never been fully comfortable addressing themselves to an elite; they have always wanted to reach a broad public. This has also been true of most major American artists, though they have interpreted the idea of accessibility in different ways. The Abstract Expressionists, for example, wanted art to be accessible through direct contact with the spectator's emotions; while the Pop artists tried to open the door through their use of images taken from popular culture.

In a narrower, more specific sense, there is a tradition of moralizing art in America. Some of the strongest representatives of this strain were the major American Regionalists of the 1930s. It sometimes surprises people when I say that, for me, one of the closest parallels for Judy Chicago's *attitudes* in the earlier history of American art is provided by Thomas Hart Benton—since Benton is often classified as a misogynist who had no use for women or for women's creativity. In fact, the resemblance between Judy Chicago and Benton is much more exact than, say, any likeness between Chicago and Georgia O'Keeffe, which is the comparison that people might instinctively choose, because Benton was a public artist.

Benton aimed to address a very broad audience on themes that he felt should be of concern to all of its members. In order to do so, he forged a style that combined aspects of modernism with things taken directly from the America he knew. He was not afraid to use things that were purely popular, long before Pop Art was invented. Experts on his work point out the links between the compositional formulae used in his murals and the way the various scenes in a narrative are organized in strip cartoons. Judy Chicago, too, has dipped into popular sources—into china painting, and, with increasing involvement, into all the wide range of skills connected with needlework. These are preeminently women's popular, democratic forms of esthetic expression. In addition, she has, in collaboration with her husband, Donald Woodman, explored possible relationships between painting and photography, which is another democratic form of image-making.

Chicago is also democratic in a different way. I have just mentioned her collaboration with her husband, which took place within the framework of the *Holocaust Project* and involved a profound, and often painful, exploration of the Jewish heritage that they both share. There have also been, from the time of *The Dinner Party* onward, collaborations with other women. Her most recent project, *Resolutions: A Stitch in Time*, involved intensive collaboration with a group of needleworkers, many of whom have now been associated with Chicago for many years. Though Chicago was certainly the initiator of the enterprise and its guiding spirit throughout, no one who has discussed it with others who worked with her can doubt that it was marked throughout by an intense spirit of sharing. The extreme virtuosity displayed in many of the pieces in the *Resolutions* sequence—something apparently contrary to the tenets of contemporary art, which sometimes seems to insist that an artwork can be original only if it is slovenly—springs directly from an American heritage of quilting bees and other forms of collaborative domestic craft.

America is a very large country—so large as not to be completely unitary. Until relatively recently, New York was so much the focus of the American art world that all other centers of artistic activity were considered to be in some way or other subordinate. This is one of the things Benton rebelled against and eventually he shook the dust of the place from his feet. Judy Chicago has never rebelled in quite the same way. Brought up a midwesterner, within a framework of secular but deeply ethical Jewish culture, she moved to California to continue her artistic education. Here, as a young artist trying to make a career, she ran up against the machismo that characterized the Los Angeles art world of the 1960s and 1970s. Other women artists submitted to the prevailing values of art; Chicago refused to do so. Through her perseverance of her own vision she eventually became the renowned figure she is today. She has been an artist with whom many American critics find it difficult to deal. Too loud, too brash, too insistent on the merits of her own point of view—and also, let's face it, too moral. A moral artist? People may eventually feel that there is, after all, nothing much wrong with that. Teaching us how to live is still one of the things that art is for.

Edward Lucie-Smith
London, England
23 August 2001

Drawing, 1950 (AGE 11)

Self-portrait: Self-loathing, 1959 (AGE 20)

ENTERING THE CULTURE
>>> JUDY CHICAGO TALKING WITH LUCY LIPPARD

JC: Not in this "postfeminist" world! (laughter)

LL: Where do you think the notion of a distinctive women's art is now?

JC: In the seventies we were guilty of a certain universalization. The notion that there was a *single* women's perspective has come in for some healthy criticism. But I think it opened the way for a more sophisticated under-standing of the ways in which diverse women's experience was filtered through race, culture, geography, sexual preference, personal experience, family structure. My view is entirely different from the mainstream art world's view, which sees "Feminist Art" as a phenomenon of the seventies that had its moment and is now passé.

LL: Even as its influence is still so clearly felt in younger women's art today.

JC: Yes. But what I've been seeing as I travel around the world is that the seventies in America and in the West ushered in a real historic change that is still not understood, because women's experience has still not entered the mainstream culture in a significant way. We gave birth to an international Feminist Art movement that is as diverse in style as the original American Feminist Art was. One of the things that got the art world crazed is that movements are usually stylistically monolithic, and this is not. This is about historic change. Mostly in developed or developing countries, women are beginning to experience esthetic freedom for the first time and consequently there is a whole range of female-centered art being created around the world. There is still no context for it in the wider culture.

On another level, in the West, what we fought for—the right of a female sensibility to be evident in art—you see it all over in younger women's art. It's just become acceptable now, and that's to be celebrated, too. But, of course, it still gets decontextualized. It doesn't get seen in the larger historic struggle for women's full parity on the planet, for women's expressive freedom, and women's right to see their work shown not only at entry level but actu-ally incorporated into the mainstream of art history, which has not yet happened. You know, the fact that there's still such small representation of women in the permanent collections and major exhibitions in mainstream institutions is an indication that the changes have taken place mostly at entry level—and those are deceptive.

LL: Decontextualization ends up being assimilation, voluntary and involuntary. Good Feminist Art is being made now and I think many of the young women artists definitely see themselves as feminists and so on. But once their work gets into the art world it's assimilated. Then it gets judged on this other weird, patriarchal level, and loses its own context, its own character. It gets neutralized.

JC: Yeah. And some young women artists whose work is definitely *antifeminist* is being confused with Feminist Art. Of course, they're the ones who are being rewarded because their art exemplifies values that are familiar to patriarchal culture. The mainstream mistakes those artists as being radical when they're really only *com-plicitous*.

I'm often asked about some of the more pernicious and misogynous images of women that pervade our museums, and there are some feminists who think those should be censored. Well, I'm not for that at all. What I'm for is a level playing field where in a museum you can see men's images of women and then you can see women's images of men. So you get to see both sides of the picture. What we have now is a *huge* amount of women's art that's simply not incorporated into the mainstream. Younger women don't even get to see it. So they always think they're doing this all by themselves for the first time.

LL: Reinventing the wheel. Same thing goes for Activist and Political Art. The education's just not there.

This morning we were talking about a show by a local women's group. They think getting together as women is a new idea, when actually what they're doing is more like those Women's Associations in the nineteenth century. They're unable to build on what's already been done.

JC: Well, that's a reflection of Gerda Lerner's point about how women exist in a state of trained ignorance, how they are raised and educated to a male-centered perspective on the world and have no access to the information that would allow them to come into consciousness. There needs to be a critique about grouping women just on the basis of being women, where there's no unifying theme except for the accident of birth. That's not enough anymore. At one historical moment in the early seventies, banding together on that basis allowed us to develop some confidence in our own points of view and to build our political strength. There was a purpose to it. Now I think it's actually counterproductive. I don't like looking at a calendar of art by women and seeing no stylistic, no philosophical, no thematic, no proactive reasons for them to be together. So even though I support women's efforts to organize as women, some critical discourse needs to take place about how they would show their art as artists.

That idea about "the center" is something else that we should go back to. Because in 1970 there was no theory, there were no women's studies classes. There wasn't anything for us as we struggled to create some kind of theoretical historical context. . . .

LL: From the practice.

JC: Right. And I think there's been both a misunderstanding and an oversimplification of what we were trying to do then. "From the center" does not necessarily mean "from the cunt." It could mean from the center of female experience.

LL: Sure. That's the way I meant it, but you were particularly associated with that idea.

JC: It got distorted to a biological notion. Now I wish I'd never coined the term "cunt imagery." Because I've had so many funny experiences, like meeting people who are doing workshops on vagina dancing and stuff like that, and I'm like . . . yeah, right. I guess it's my own fault, but I was never thinking about the cunt as only the vulva. I was thinking about the cunt in a metaphysical way, if one can say that. Like what does it mean to be organized around a center core? How does that change your experience? For example, women are more comfortable going to doctors for physicals than men are, because women are used to being entered, and they're used to the fact that their bodies are not a total boundary. That dramatically changes your relationship to the world, your relationship to other people.

LL: I'll stick to a lot of the things I said in the seventies, one of which is that women's experience biologically, socially, sexually, politically is different from men's, so the art that emerges from that experience is bound to be different. We don't harp on the visual differences the way we used to and we don't oversimplify them the way we did at one point, but they're still there and they're still valid content for women's work.

JC: As many times as feminist theorists posit the notion that gender is a changing construct, the fact remains that it's *not* for most women. Being female dramatically shapes and often limits their experience. When you're in the ivory tower of the academy, it's one thing to think about women's experience on a totally theoretical basis. It's another thing to deal with women's lived experience, and in that gap, it seems to me, is where the work needs to be done. There has to be some greater web of understanding between the theoretical and the real.

LL: Absolutely. That's exactly what we went through with Activist Art in New York in the eighties. We read the theorists, but the theorists never looked seriously, *theoretically,* at anything we were doing as we tried to theorize through practice. It used to just piss me off so, that abyss between theory and practice.

JC: Yes—the idea that theory can exist independent from practice has really been hurting the women's studies courses, in general. Young women study women as if they weren't one. Actually it's been very interesting to me to be teaching again, because I've had a number of women's studies students in my classes. When they begin to actually make art, to practice the theory, they come in touch with the difficulties—the gap between theory and practice, the fact that their lived experience is often not consistent with the theory they've been studying. So the idea that gender is a changing construct is very interesting to debate, but then they have to confront the degree to which they've been conditioned as women against action. I understand theorists get really pissed at the suggestion that theory is not action.

LL: Well, ideas *can* be a form of action, in collaboration with or in consideration of direct action. But they need to be communicated first. The theorists' vocabularies alone throw up tremendous barriers between thought and action. For a while that represented an advance over "old-fashioned feminism," but I think it was self-defeating in the long run.

JC: Many young women don't want to identify with feminism. Even though I wish this weren't the case, I do understand it from my own experience. Because when I was a student at UCLA, there were two tenured female professors in the studio department, from the earlier waves of feminism. One of them had a collection of women's art, which I thought was just so quaint! I couldn't understand why anybody would do that, and I wanted nothing to do with these women because I had been brought up with the idea that what women did was less significant than what men did, and therefore I should identify with the men. I had been identifying with male art history since I was a child, and even though I had some level of nascent political consciousness—as you did, too, when you were young—if I tried to bring up any issues of gender discrimination, I would be put down with this thing, "What are you, some kind of suffragette?" Which was an earlier form of, "What are you, some kind of feminist?"

These terms become very effectively demonized by the mainstream as an effort, again, to insure that young women will continue to identify with male history. My feeling about young women's resistance to the term *feminism* is that here's the good news: We opened up a larger area of practice for them; they are not encountering discrimination as early as we did. The bad news is that they are not coming to consciousness. And the world has not changed significantly in terms of male domination. It has to do with not feeling represented at all.

LL: Well, I'm so far out of the art world now that I don't really have an overview. I'm not sure how the day-to-day life of a young woman artist happens today.

JC: I'm not just talking about the art world. Young women in general continue to tell me that they have very few female mentors. They rarely study women in art or art history. And even when there's an effort, as there has been in a number of departments, to bring women into studio teaching (and there are departments that have made big efforts that are a third or more women now) there's still a bias in the curriculum. The way it works is that most women and men teaching art do not know the history of women's art. Therefore, when they look at young women's work, even if they intend to be supportive, they cannot identify nascent impulses in that work that would be familiar if they knew the history of women's art.

That's why it's so easy for me, because I've spent so much time immersed in the history of women's art and women's historic struggle that I can recognize the earliest stages of attempts to articulate something about their own experience—molestation, rape, whatever. I'm not as good with young men, but the opposite is true for most male and many female professors.

LL: I remember writing in the old days about schools intentionally hiring women with no consciousness, so they could say they had a woman, and not get anything accomplished.

JC: It's amazing how they find so many.

LL: A line of yours in the '74 interview that always stuck with me was about how women have so far been unable to transform our circumstances into our subject matter because we've been so embedded in our circumstances, instead of using them to reveal the whole human condition.

JC: I think to some extent that's changed. Katha Pollitt wrote a really interesting piece in the *New York Times* about the contemporary view of feminism, and the tremendous overemphasis on the personal. She used the phrase "feminism, *c'est moi*." Even though there was an important period when women artists began to replace their personal experiences with larger meaning, a lot of work by young women now—particularly images of women as victims—I find suffocating, overly narcissistic. Now women are allowed to deal openly with themselves as subjects, but that can be as much of a trap as *not* being able to deal with yourself as a subject. Because the self becomes the world. That's a very dangerous area for women.

LL: This personal growth movement, whatever they call it, has exacerbated the ignorance about the "personal is political" aspect of feminism. The fact is that it works both ways. The political is personal, too.

JC: Women are always too willing to change themselves. It's easier than trying to change the world. One can actually have the illusion that one is doing something important. Don't get me wrong. I think personal growth is important, just not as an end in itself. Women's broader growth is not supported. Actually, the whole world of needlework and needlework kits is an incredible metaphor for the larger world of women, where women's abilities are short-changed and their expectations are undermined. A woman with great talent is given a paint-by-number kit and subject matter that is irrelevant to her life. That's why I've enjoyed subverting needlework so much, and providing needleworkers with images that have meaning, with the ability to use their skills at a level of excellence. To rise instead of to fall. But women are encouraged to fall.

LL: Or simply to maintain the status quo. Do you see a lot of social activism among these young women?

JC: No.

LL: I often do when I'm lecturing on cultural activism. Young people run up afterward and say here's what we're doing and we want to do this or that. It's like there's a deep need to be acting on our ideals but so little framework, so little education, so little encouragement, so few models.

JC: Oh, I agree with that. If you give them the opportunity, it's quite astonishing. But there's so little opportunity. Some years ago we heard Elie Wiesel speak in a university. The question and answer period was really very moving because at one point, after hearing question after question from these young people, he said, "How is it that I, who have seen the worst in life, have hope, and you, who have your whole life before you, feel so hopeless?"

There's a feeling out there that nothing can be changed. That's why Jim Jeffords's rejection of the right-wing Republican Party [in May 2001] was so tremendous. It was a public act symbolizing that one individual can really make a difference.

LL: You've talked about expanding our understanding of the human condition by adding a female perspective, and it seems like that's been the driving force behind your work for many years now.

JC: Well, my goal has been to mine my own experience as a Jewish female person, an American person, to go from that particular to the larger human experience. Along the way, my work has become more modest in size and scale, though maybe not in underlying intention. As one grows as a human being, one is humbled by recognizing one's place in the larger world—you know, something I didn't have when I was young.

JC: But working on the Holocaust humbled me—as did beginning to understand women's experience in a larger global context of oppression and injustice, realizing the degree to which we have to be committed to a just world . . . a really just world. It's not enough for some people in America to have opportunities. All people have to have opportunities. That's the goal of feminism, and it's been tremendously distorted. That's why I think "postfeminism" is such an unbelievable conceit. When I get asked questions about it I say, "This is what feminism imagines: a world of justice and equity, where everybody has a chance." And then I say, "Do we live in that world? No. Is this a postfeminist world? No. *That* would be a postfeminist world."

LL: That's a great line.

JC: It's so interesting, historically, to have been in two identity movements, both women and Jews. One could say that the subtext of the *Holocaust Project* was what does it mean to be Jewish in a post-Holocaust world? There's so much work now being done on Jewish identity. And it's so interesting that when people want to organize exhibitions on Jewish art, one hears exactly the same thing we used to hear when trying to organize exhibitions on women's art: "Oh, I don't want to show only with other Jewish artists. I don't want to be seen as a Jewish artist." Sound familiar?

I've been universalizing from my own experience with the caveat that I understand that even the term *universal* is not accurate because at this moment we really don't *have* a universal human experience. Culture so shapes and mediates women's experience. Sexuality, for instance. An infibulated woman's sexuality is entirely different from an emancipated Western woman's sexuality, or from that of a religious woman who's been raised with the idea of sex as sin.

Which brings us to *Resolutions*, because in its modest way that's actually what I was interested in. The needlepoints on human rights are very playful. There are six proverbs, but the underlying issue is that as a human species on the planet we don't have even a fundamental agreement about basic human rights. Sometimes I describe *Resolutions* as a response to William Bennett's *Book of Virtues*, which irked me no end. Things *are* wrong in our culture, it's just that the Right's solutions are so retrograde, particularly for women. I thought it would be interesting to try to look at some of the same issues and come up with an alternative vision of what to do about them. Of course, *Resolutions* is already culture-bound by the fact that they're English proverbs. On the other hand, one has to start somewhere, and for better or for worse, English is probably as close as we've come to a universal language, spoken pretty well all over the developed world. It's cultural imperialism, but it's a fact.

LL: I use Spanish/New Mexican *dichos* (sayings) now and then in my community newsletter, and sometimes I really have to work to understand what their message is, because they're coming from such a different place. . . . Let's talk about *The Dinner Party*. How has that fared in twenty-two years? Do you see it differently now? Do you think it's seen differently now that it's a "feminist icon"?

JC: If you ask me, its iconic status has resulted both in its widespread influence and its lack of permanent housing for more than two decades. It symbolizes the gap between the level of changes and real change, because its long period of "homelessness" indicated that there is some fundamental resistance to incorporating women's symbology and iconography into the mainstream cultural *thrust* . . . so to speak.

Also, it helps that I can see my own struggle in the larger struggle for equity for women, in and out of the arts. It took a hundred years before there was sufficient interest in Mary Cassatt's work to mount a major retrospective. Imagine what it would have meant to us in terms of our understanding of women's esthetic achievements if we had been able to see and study Mary Cassatt's sixty-five-foot mural from the 1893 Woman's Building, portraying women passing down the fruits of knowledge to their daughters—probably the first major feminist work of art, actually, or woman-centered work of art. The fact that it was lost to history allowed Mary Cassatt to be portrayed as Degas's student. Its presence would have posed a constant challenge to that idea. These losses have to stop. And women can stop them.

LL: What do you want to see in women's museums?

JC: I want to see the art of those women who in *all* circumstances were able to assert their humanity, whether that's women making pots in a culture where only men made pots, or women making baskets, or keeping a tradition alive in the face of all kinds of obstacles, when the mainstream culture was out to destroy the culture itself. Oppositional art, that's what I'm interested in. Like the self-portrait with the little inscription saying, "I Catharina van Hemessen painted myself." She speaks across the centuries to us, telling us that even in the bleakest moments of history a woman could see herself in opposition to the cultural messages and claim her own humanity. I want to see art that affirms us as women and as human beings. That's what's missing from our institutions. That's why so many people flock to my shows—no matter how hard the art world tries to prevent them from seeing my art. Whenever it appears, thousands of people turn out because of that hunger for different voices. It's like that question they keep on raising: "Why have there been no great women artists?" I'm sorry, that's an oxymoron. The question is why have there been so many great women artists we don't know about?

Part of the answer lies in the issue of content, because it is in content that women's art is often different. Nobody knows what to do with content-based art. There's no way to deal with art on the Holocaust without confronting the content. I think that that's one of the biggest problems I've had as an artist is that my art is content-based, in an art world that doesn't want content to intrude, to bother you, to distress you. Content should be a quiet little person in the corner, maybe the subtext, but certainly not the center of the work.

LL: So your art is accused of being too literal and illustrational. What's wrong with literalism and illustration?

JC: Most of what's been said about my work is not rational. I've decided it's sort of fantastic that I'm going on sixty-two and the critics are still foaming at the mouth. Most artists my age are like ho-hum. This means my work is still vital and still dealing with things that make people uncomfortable. . . . "A Chicken in Every Pot" is no more illustrative than Grant Wood's *American Gothic*—the image it's based on. So why isn't that word used pejoratively with him?

LL: It often is. Along with Thomas Hart Benton. . .

JC: I was sort of shocked by Edward Lucie-Smith's associating me with Benton.

LL: I thought it made sense—something about the fluidity of his figures.

JC: I only understood the Thomas Hart Benton thing because I saw the Indiana murals. His use of symbolic figures is very close to what I've done. In the *Holocaust Project*, in the transport images, for example, each one of those figures is based on actual stories that I read about the experiences of the transport to the camps. They're not a particular person; they symbolize a particular experience.

LL: Do you ever get homesick for the abstract art you were making before we peeled back the . . .

JC: It's all your fault, too. I hope you realize that. . . . Well, there's beginning to be a reassessment of some of that early work of mine in retrospect. They couldn't see it at the time, you know? Like my early work from the seventies, which I couldn't get shown anywhere. You remember that?

LL: All too well. That time you were staying with us in New York and taking a portfolio around to the galleries. . .

JC: I was incredibly naïve. I was like from outer space. I really believed in all these things like truth and justice and beauty and a better world. I didn't understand greed, jealousy, competition, how the art world worked. So it was like Little Miss Naïve confronting the real world. That's why I feel it's so important to prepare young women for what's coming . . . and young men, too. But as hard as it was, would you change one thing about your life? I wouldn't.

LL: God, no. Me either. . . How do you think your form language has changed over the years?

JC: Well, first of all, almost unbeknownst to me, in the process of creating *The Dinner Party*, I went back to being a representational artist. You know, when I was young I was classically trained and all that. I started doing sort of more abstract work in graduate school, partly because that was the language of the time.

LL: You were good at it and you got a lot of approval from it.

JC: Oh, no, I did not.

LL: Well, you were in the *Primary Structures* show, and that was a really important moment.

JC: Yeah, right, but that was after huge resistance on the part of the West Coast people. It was a miracle I got in that show. It's because I had a good dealer. And I didn't understand the meaning of getting in that show. I should have gotten on the plane and gone to New York and gotten a gallery. But I was still hurting from Walter Hobbs refusing to look at the piece and the West Coast people not taking me seriously. See, I always had a sense that my work was good. When *The Dinner Party* opened in Chicago, I took my high school art teacher from The Art Institute around to see it, and it was really a wonderful moment. He said, "Judy, I always knew you were going to do something important." Well, I always knew it, too, but I would never say it because I was a girl and you just didn't say those things. I had no idea where I was going, you know. I just went. And I didn't know when I was doing *The Dinner Party* that I was going back to representation, primarily on the back of the needlework, the runners.

That's the way my work has evolved over the years. I specifically choose the technique and I choose the form I use for the content I'm exploring. I used to say I'd work in bubble gum if that was the appropriate form. There's been a lot of misunderstanding about the way I work. Working on the *Holocaust Project* or the *Birth Project*, there was no way I was going to be abstract; the subjects called for representational images. Also, designing for needlework (except for embroidery) requires a generalization of form. Some people don't understand that, so they say I can't draw, which is ridiculous. When you design, particularly for the grid of needlepoint, you have to generalize or you can't make a form come alive. I'm capable of drawing the most detailed images as well, and I go back and forth based on what the subject matter requires.

When I was working on the *Holocaust Project*, I wanted the images to be rooted in the reality of the historic event, so I incorporated photography. The painting had to be so detailed or it wouldn't merge with the photography. I wasn't painting on top of the photography; Donald and I were actually inventing ways technically to *merge* painting and photography. Merging is very important in my work—in some of the images like *Fleshgardens*—the merging of flesh and landscape. Or in the *Atmospheres* [pyrotechnic environments] merging color and landscape, and in the airbrush paintings where I merged color and surface. So what's that about? It's about breaking down boundaries, breaking down hierarchies, breaking down false barriers. These are philosophical impulses expressed visually and esthetically. So by the time I got to *Resolutions*, I wanted to really make much more exquisite images. I designed the *Birth Project* for a lower level of skill, because it was so democratized and there were so many hundreds of people trying to participate. In *Resolutions*, I wanted to reclaim that process, go farther and render each image at the highest level possible. Edward Lucie-Smith was right when he said that my impulse in *Resolutions* was to finally make needlework a fine art.

LL: I liked the *Now or Never* piece, which seemed abstract in a sense and reminded me of your old work in the mid-seventies, like the *Great Ladies*.

JC: I never actually thought about that until you said it, but it's the same woman doing the art, you know. Actually, *Now or Never* was dictated by a needlework kit design. The woman who worked on it brought it to me and I got a big kick out of appropriating that kit and transforming it.

LL: But also, out of all the so-called craft mediums that you've worked in, that you could have gone on with, you chose needlework. It's a Finish Fetish kind of medium—*extremely* detailed and perfectionist. . . . You can't screw around with needlework, can you?

JC: No. You know, there's something that has never been discussed in terms of the choices I made and the directions I took. I didn't want to stop doing china painting or working in porcelain. I wanted to make a porcelain room for *The Dinner Party*. I wanted to extend those plates into a major architectural piece. I'd seen those incredible porcelain rooms in Europe, and I wanted to do a modern version—painted porcelain outdoor sculptures and fountains, stuff like that. But I've never gotten support for that level of ambition. I stopped doing the *Atmospheres* because I couldn't get funding to fill the Grand Canyon. Seriously!

LL: The elusiveness and the total dematerialization of the *Atmospheres* was an interesting direction. But you wouldn't really want to put your time and energy into that now, would you?

JC: No, probably not. One of the reasons that so many women have done performance work and ephemeral work is specifically because it's ephemeral. There's been less resistance. If I'd gotten funding to do major outdoor sculpture or big fireworks pieces, I might have gone in a whole different direction. When I was able to create an atelier situation for *The Dinner Party*, it allowed me to expand my art-making to the level that I was capable of doing. That was the first time, and I could never have done it without that particular moment in time when so many people wanted to help me make this monument to women's history. I'm not the kind of artist who just works by herself in a corner. I have an expansive vision, and it involves many people. In order to be able to enhance that, I had to go where there was support. And there were hundreds of needleworkers who wanted to work with me.

LL: And it was enough of a cottage industry that it was feasible without tremendous funding.

JC: Exactly. In *Resolutions* we all paid for ourselves; we just split the cost of each piece. We own each work jointly. Needleworkers are used to spending a certain amount of money on the materials they need. It was when I was working on *The Dinner Party* that I discovered that I had this ability to design for needlework, which was a miracle, since I can't sew or stitch.

LL: I just had this flash of us sitting in New York years ago. You were sewing on a button and I was sewing patches on Ethan's denim jacket, and we were in hysterics at this mutually inept domestic scene. Anyway, you've always had a terrifically sensuous relationship to your materials.

JC: You know, I've been doing watercolors for several years. The L.A. architect and art collector Elyse Grinstein gave me a set of watercolors and said, "Here, loosen up." Actually it was very amusing because I started using them while I was traveling. I did this little tiny book called *More Than a Hundred Drawings*. This was right after we moved to Belen. So I enrolled in a watercolor class at the local college under a pseudonym. I just took my assistant's name and had her enroll for me. I left after I had learned what was useful, the tools and the implements and all that stuff.

You know, there's a series you've never seen—140 drawings in a year called *Autobiography of a Year*. I worked on that for a year—not just the drawings—I worked on the particular problem of trying to get a pure impulse on the page in a very direct way. Watercolor doesn't allow a lot of extended working. You have to put down what you mean pretty quickly. Over the six years of *Resolutions* I did several series of works: *Autobiography of a Year, Thinking About Trees, Los Lunas Hills*, and I'm still doing watercolors. I may have finally cured myself of that long, indirect process. Watercolor seems to be all I'm interested in doing now. I love its transparency, its delicacy. I feel like I'm just going to spend my dotage doing it.

LL: I was going to ask you about the *Los Lunas Hills*, your only purely landscape series. Do you think New Mexico has affected your work at all? You've always been involved with light. . . .

JC: No, I don't think so. The *Hills* were the first time I did something like that. When I decided I wanted to learn watercolor, we kept passing the Los Lunas Hill, and we used to hike up on it. I thought it was beautiful, and for me, the best way for me to learn something is by practice. I took photographs of the hill at different times of the day and night, and I'd observe it. I looked at it from the east, the west, the north, the south. And I remember Stuart Ashman, who was then the director of Santa Fe's Museum of Fine Arts, saying that somebody had come up to him after the landscape show opened at Arlene LewAllen's gallery and said, "What's Judy doing, becoming O'Keeffe?" And he said, "You don't understand; that's purely Judy, the examination, the thoughtfulness, the way she broke down the hill, looked at it from different points of view. That is not O'Keeffe."

LL: What about this series called *Cat Erotica*? I'm curious about that. Is it erotic for the cats or for you?

JC: I showed it in L.A. in my works on paper show recently, and at the opening this woman came up to me and she said, "Where do you get a cat like *that*?"

LL: Who are the audiences you want particularly to reach?

JC: In the seventies, I was specifically rethinking the issue of audience and trying to consider a female audience as my target audience. And, of course, most art museum audiences *are* female, but the art is not conceived with them in mind. Over the years my audience has just grown and diversified, so now I feel that my audience is whoever comes with an open mind. I have a big audience among feminists, of course, but also in the gay and lesbian community, among environmentalists, animal rights people, the liberal Jewish community, needleworkers. *Resolutions* brought more people into the Skirball Museum in Los Angeles than they've ever had in their museum, and it was diverse. It's very gratifying to have such a big audience, but it's an audience that I've built.

LL: Yes, absolutely. It's a unique situation in contemporary art. You've talked about art as a way of communicating cultural experience to an audience. Do you think it's really possible to cross over, and how does art do that? Have black women, for instance, responded to your *Black and Radiant* from *Song of Songs*?

JC: If it's not possible to cross over, then human effort over the centuries would be an entire waste. Do I think it's a perfect communication? No. I think people have to get over their idea that white women's art is only for white women and African Americans' art is only for African Americans and lesbians' art is only for lesbians. That's a very pernicious idea. Art from one human experience to another can imperfectly transcend some of the barriers between us.

LL: Which brings us to the pitfalls of identity politics. I always find myself defending identity politics, even though I know that when you take it one step too far, it ends up nationalist or even Nazi. At the same time, identity is deeply important to many people as a way of finding themselves and their place in the world—a base they can fight back from and act from. It's a politicization of experience.

JC: Identity politics becomes nasty when it becomes exclusive. The missing word in identity politics is the word human. There are common aspects to our experience and there are unique aspects to our experience. And negotiating those is, of course, the challenge. It's much easier to take on a defensive posture and bury oneself in self. I've spoken to some administrators at some of the major universities in the country. They're just beside themselves about the degree to which identity politics is destroying some of the programs. It has become tremendously acrimonious. And nobody seems to know quite what to do about it.

LL: It was supposed to be expansive, to educate others from a base of strength, and it's often turned out to be defensive and incestuous. . . . Anyway, let's talk a little about your process. Is there a rhythm where you do a big collaborative project, and then you go back to the studio for a while? Do you have any other big projects in the works now?

JC: No, I don't think I'm going to do any more.

LL: Really? But didn't you say that before *Resolutions,* too?

JC: Well, *Resolutions* started out very modestly and playfully. But even all through *Resolutions* I was also doing individual work, and I think the only time that dynamic didn't happen was during *The Dinner Party,* when I was so overwhelmed with work, and towards the end of the *Holocaust Project.* Needlework is slow. After a couple years the *Birth Project* got to a point where I put it on a more regular basis for reviewing and stuff like that. Then I began to have downtime and I started working on *Powerplay* and I was going back and forth between the *Birth Project* and *Powerplay* and then between *Powerplay* and the *Holocaust Project.* It's important to understand that my process, even when I'm working on a major project, is to do inquiries into the various aspects of that project on paper. I think through things by making art. So there's dozens or even hundreds of drawings that back up each of the projects.

Also there have been many times in my life when personal things happened or relationships broke up, and I just haven't known what to do. For example, after *The Dinner Party* showed in San Francisco and it was such a huge success, then all the museums canceled and I lost everything. I just didn't know what else to do except go back in the studio. When I couldn't solve things, the solution was to work. And so I don't see a big distinction between my major projects and my personal work. There's a continuum.

LL: Why was *Resolutions* a collaborative project? Because it seemed to me that you could have had just as much fun and maybe more freedom if you'd been in the studio making a series of paintings on that subject.

JC: I definitely wanted to use needlework, I wanted to go farther with the merging of painting and needlework than I had done before, and I wanted to subvert tradition: needlework tradition and kit tradition and the tradition of proverbs in kits. I wanted to bend them to mean something other than what they originally meant. It just seemed like the right way to do it was with needlework, softening the message, the meaning, through the technique. *Resolutions* may be playful and small, but people get deceived by its simplicity. My work is never simple—not conceptually, philosophically, technically. Maybe it's that Finish Fetish thing. I like it to look as if it was effortless, but behind that is just a whole complex of thinking. It's one of the reasons people spend so much time in my shows. This assumption of simple images prevents some of the more sophisticated art world people from understanding how complex my work is. It seems like it's the *less* sophisticated lookers who see more.

LL: I was thinking about content-based work and how it's asked to carry an awful lot of weight. A lot of people don't expect content in art and don't get it when they see it. There are a lot of sophisticated artists who talk about their content, you know, and there's this in it and there's that in it and I'm thinking, *Yeah? Where?*

JC: There's a difference between intellectual content and philosophical content. Intellectual content is about the relationship of the government to torture. It's very detached from the experience of the artist. The image doesn't necessarily seem to have a lot to do with the supposed intellectual content. Then it becomes indecipherable. I know how to make art like that. I made art like that. But I deliberately set out to unlearn that. I wanted to find a way to more fully unite the meaning of the work with the final image, so that it didn't get lost in some set of intellectualizations along the way, so I wasn't the only one who understood the metaphor or the form. I find that alienating and destructive to the art impulse, and to the art community in the long run. Because unless we broaden our audience, unless we help people understand why art is important to their lives, we're going to continue to be under assault—even though at the same time more people than ever go to museums. One wonders what they're going to museums *for*.

LL: Museum-going has always been a kind of upwardly mobile activity. Do you still have any hope for alternatives to the commercial mainstream art world, given what you've just said? So much has been tried over the years, and though these examples are out there, very few artists seem to know about them or care to emulate them. I was thinking of the time you and I and Diane Gelon [*The Dinner Party* administrator, now a lawyer] were sitting around trying to figure out what to do with *The Dinner Party*. You'd just gotten the bad news that nobody was going to show it, and we were talking about setting up an alternative system, and that's really how it finally got shown around the world, through an alternative network.

JC: That's something you and I always disagreed about. Even though I support alternative voices and alternative structures, in terms of strategies against exclusion, I've always wanted to see our *institutions* expand to accommodate diverse voices. Women own half of public space. I want to see women and a diversity of voices in public space in proportion to who we are and what we've done. That's going to take a really long time because institutional change is glacial. It seems to me that one of the big challenges of our generation (and our time is rapidly running out) is to translate the changes in consciousness into real institutional change. That's what I've always been interested in. I was very involved in creating alternative structures, but they were never an end in themselves. They were ways of opening up space, of pressuring the mainstream institutions. They were a way of forcing society to recognize the richness of the cultural artifacts and practice that was going on around it. Women belong in the mainstream institutions and we belong in the mainstream of culture. Until that happens we have to have many, many alternative institutions. But the goal has to be transforming our culture and our cultural practices.

Galisteo, New Mexico
29 May 2001

EARLY CALIFORNIA YEARS

>>> 1964–1971

When I was a young artist in the burgeoning Los Angeles scene, I wanted, above all, to be taken seriously in an art world that had no conception of or room for feminine sensibility. In an effort to fit in, I accommodated my esthetic impulses to the prevailing modernist style.

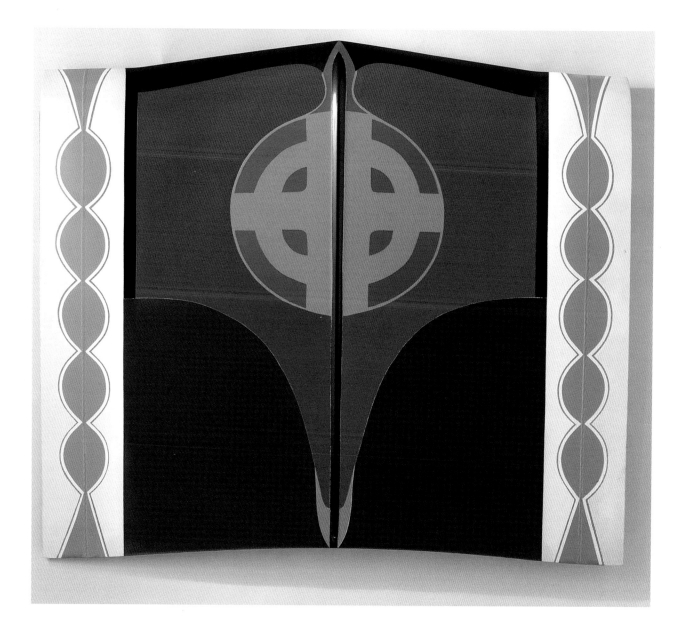

Car Hood, 1964

Mother Superette, 1964

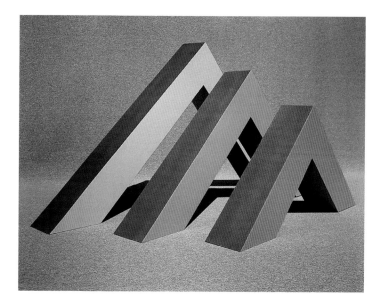

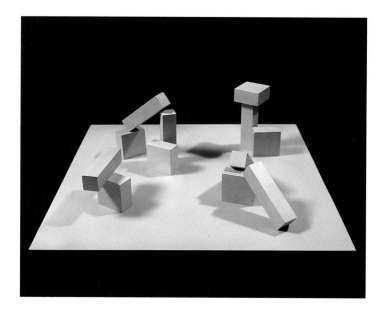

Trinity, 1965
Aluminum Game Board, 1965

Bronze Domes, 1968

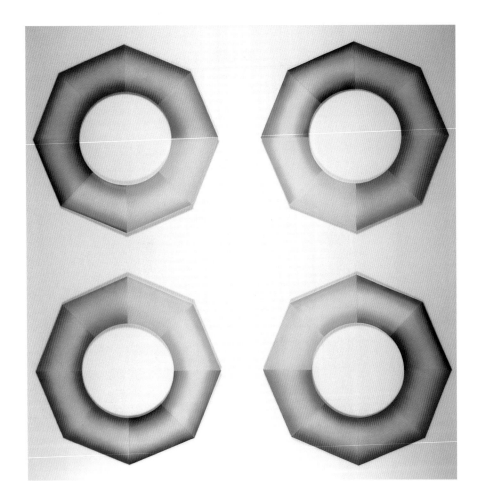

Pasadena Lifesavers–Red Series #4, 1969–1970

Sky Flesh, FROM THE *Fleshgarden* SERIES, 1971

BREAKTHROUGH YEARS

>>> 1972–1975

After struggling for a decade in a male-dominated art community, I decided to take the risk of being who I was as an artist and as a woman. I attempted to reconcile my personal subject matter and style with a formalist visual language. Finally, I threw off those earlier, more abstracted methods in favor of a clearer and more accessible imagery.

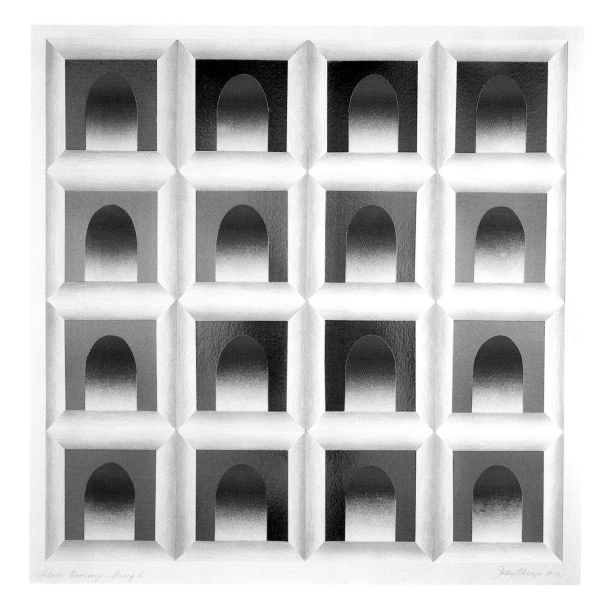

Silver Doorways (PROOF E), 1972

Christina of Sweden, FROM THE *Great Ladies* SERIES, 1972

Elizabeth, in Honor of Elizabeth, FROM THE *Great Ladies* SERIES, 1973

Marie Antoinette, FROM THE *Great Ladies* SERIES, 1973

Transformation Drawing—Great Ladies Changing into Butterflies, 1973

Into the Darkness   Judy Chicago '73

Through the Flower, (Into the Darkness), 1973

Through the Flower, 1973

35

Let It All Hang Out, 1973

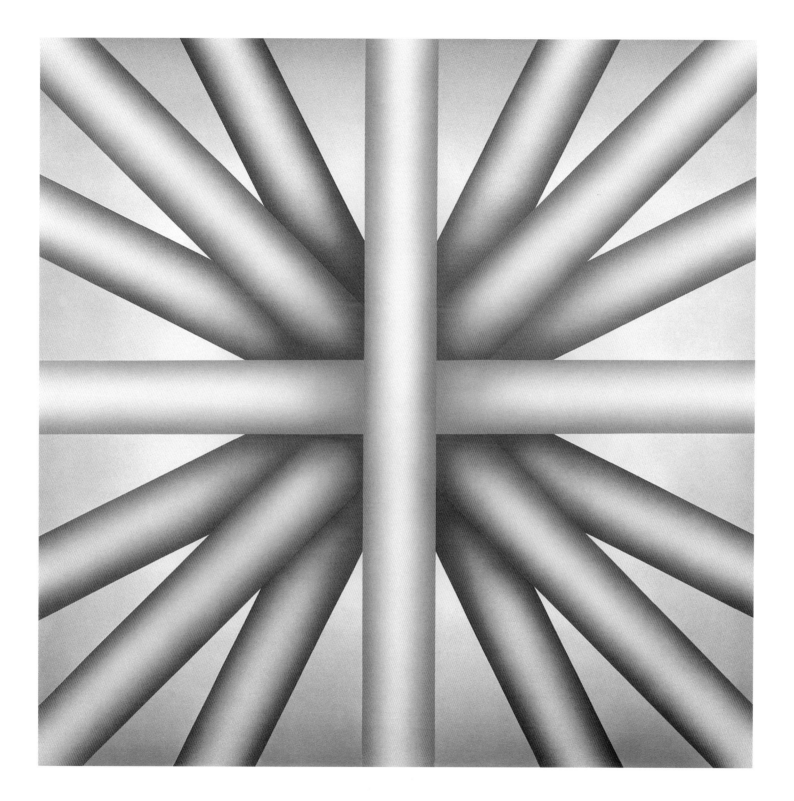

Heaven Is for White Men Only, 1973

How does it feel to be rejected?

In November, 1973, I went to Chicago for my husband's opening. I had always wanted to have a show there as it is my home town, so I was a bit jealous that Lloyd was showing there first. Nonetheless, I was happy for him and in a good mood when we went to a party afterwards, given by some local collectors. Several of my cousins went with us. When we were leaving, I shook hands with the host and thanked him for having us. "I haven't had you yet", he said. I flushed and stuttered, "Thank you for spoiling my evening".

On the same trip, an artist friend of mine took me to see a gallery owner who, she thought, would be interested in my work. When he saw my slides, he offered me a show in the Spring and requested that I send him two paintings when my show in L.A. was over. My family was very excited about my having a show in Chicago. When he received the paintings, he called and asked me to bring some drawings on my next trip. In January, I arrived at the gallery, unwrapped my drawings and then, he informed me that when he saw my paintings, he had not had any response to them. He did not even look at the drawings. I picked up my work and left.

It's like having your flower split open.

Chicago Rejection Drawing   Judy Chicago 1974

Female Rejection Drawing #1 (How Does It Feel to Be Rejected?), 1974

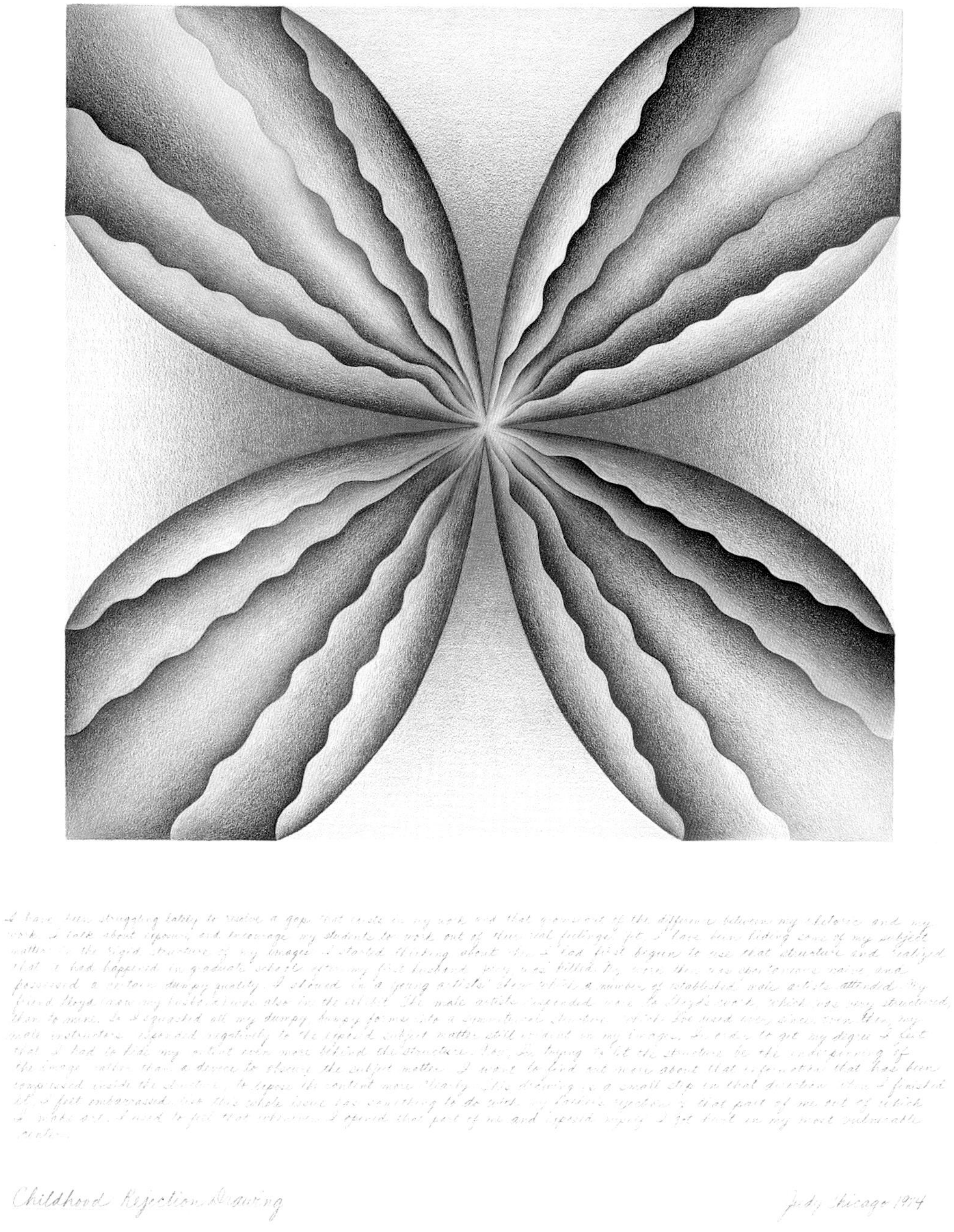

Female Rejection Drawing #2 (Childhood Rejection), 1974

Female Rejection Drawing #3 (Peeling Back), 1974

Female Rejection Drawing #4 (Rejection Fantasy), 1974

How does it feel to expose your real identity?

These images are what I've been dealing with all along in my work and hiding behind a formalized structure. Not only was I afraid to reveal the real subject matter of my work, but I didn't know how to draw these images before. I could only draw a vaginal form or symbolize that form. In this drawing, the cunt transmutes into a cave and then into a metamorphosing butterfly, wanting to be born and wiggle out of its old skin. For the last two weeks, I hardly left my studio. I worked 12-14 hours a day on this picture.

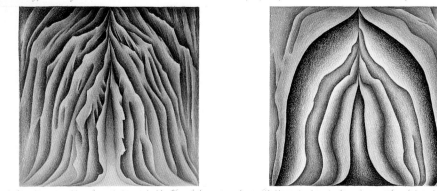

During the time I was working, I went deeper inside than I have ever been. At the end of each day, I was exhausted and shaken by the struggle to go beyond the "cunt" that I revealed in the "peeling back" drawing. In these images, I discarded my formalized structure for the first time and in so doing, broke through into a new form language, one that will allow me to make clear images of my experience as a woman. But, in breaking through, I became frightened by the prospect of my new loneliness and the difficulty of going on from here.

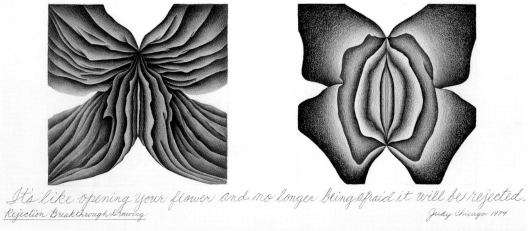

It's like opening your flower and no longer being afraid it will be rejected.

Rejection Breakthrough Drawing   Judy Chicago 1974

Female Rejection Drawing #5 (How Does It Feel to Expose Your Real Identity?), 1974

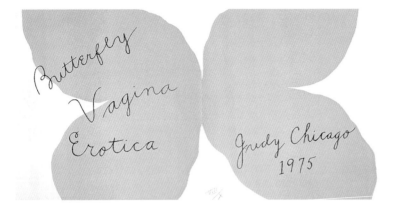

Butterfly Vagina Erotica, 1975

Did You Know Your Mother Had a Sacred Heart?, 1976

THE DINNER PARTY YEARS

>>> 1974–1979

Having discovered my rich and previously unknown heritage as a woman, I set out to convey what I believed would be potentially empowering information to a broad and diverse audience through a monumental work of art that symbolized the history of women in Western civilization.

The Dinner Party, INSTALLATION VIEW, 1979

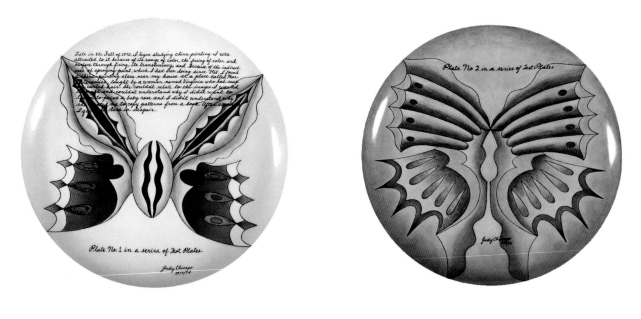

all in all, I worked on 6 Butterfly Plates on and off for a year and a half. In the last firing, one of the plates was ruined and one came out in a way that I didn't like. But, that happened after I had already numbered some of the plates, all of which aptly demonstrates the slow, difficult, frustrating process of china-painting. While I was going through this process, Miriam Schapiro was undergoing a rather devastating divorce. We often talked while we painted and the class consisted of an ongoing exchange of technical and emotional information. By the time the lessons ended, her name was no longer Schapiro as she had taken back her maiden name of Halpern, but ending twenty years of marriage

Plate No. 5 in a series of Test Plates

Judy Chicago
1973/74

ABOVE AND ABOVE LEFT: JUDY CHICAGO IN THE CHINA PAINTING STUDIO, CIRCA 1974

The Dinner Party BANNERS, 1979

INSTALLATION FOR *The Dinner Party* BANNERS, 1996

Hypatia, STUDY FOR RUNNER BACK, 1979

Illuminated Letter for Hypatia

jc '77

Hypatia, STUDY FOR ILLUMINATED LETTER, 1977

Hypatia, TEST PLATE, 1979

RIGHT: *The Dinner Party* (detail), 1979, HYPATIA PLACE SETTING

Eleanor of Aquitaine, TEST PLATE, 1979

Eleanor of Aquitaine, GRIDDED RUNNER DRAWING, 1979

55

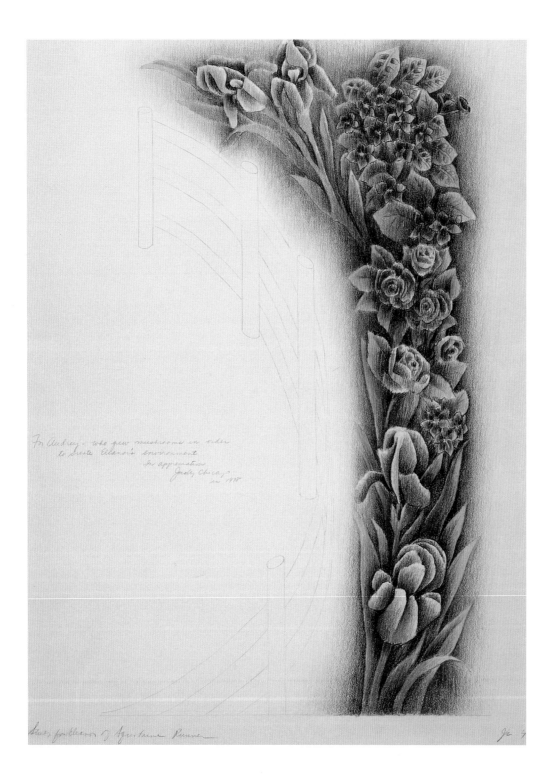

Eleanor of Aquitaine, STUDY FOR RUNNER, 1977   RIGHT: *The Dinner Party* (detail), 1979, ELEANOR OF AQUITAINE PLACE SETTING

Eleanor
of Aquitaine

of Champa
Virgin Mary

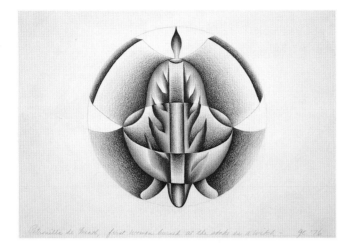

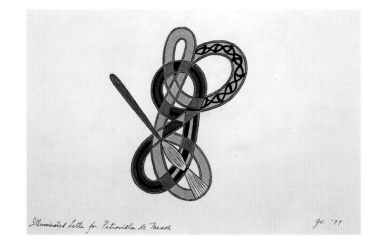

Petronilla de Meath, PLATE DRAWING, 1976

Petronilla de Meath, TEST PLATE, 1979

Petronilla de Meath, STUDY FOR ILLUMINATED LETTER, 1977

RIGHT: *The Dinner Party* (detail), 1979, PETRONILLA DE MEATH PLACE SETTING

Mary Wollstonecraft, TEST PLATE, 1979

Mary Wollstonecraft, GRIDDED RUNNER DRAWING, 1979
RIGHT: *The Dinner Party* (detail), 1979, MARY WOLLSTONECRAFT PLACE SETTING

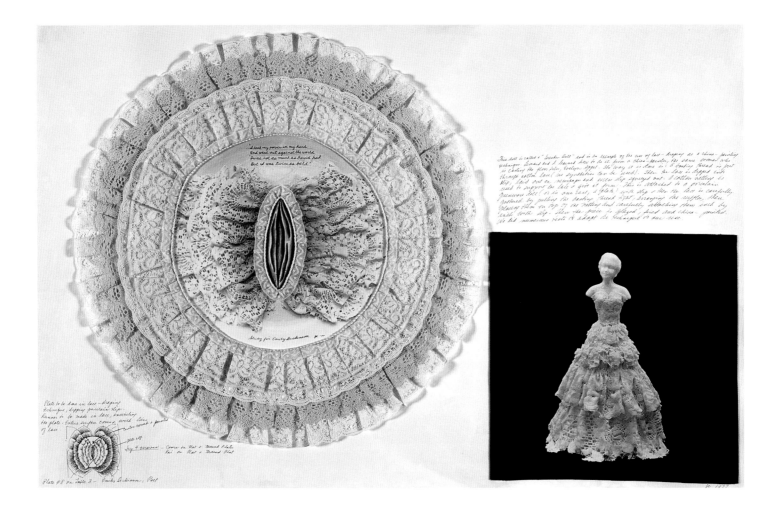

Emily Dickinson, STUDY FOR PLATE, 1977   RIGHT: *The Dinner Party* (detail), 1979, EMILY DICKINSON PLACE SETTING

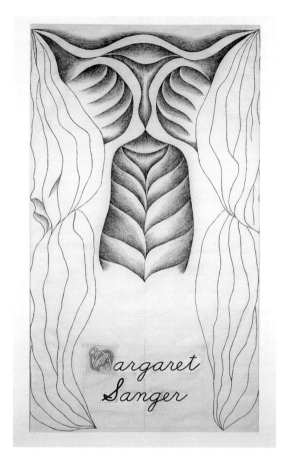

Margaret Sanger, TEST PLATE, 1979

Margaret Sanger, GRIDDED RUNNER DRAWING, 1979
RIGHT: *The Dinner Party* (detail), 1979, MARGARET SANGER PLACE SETTING

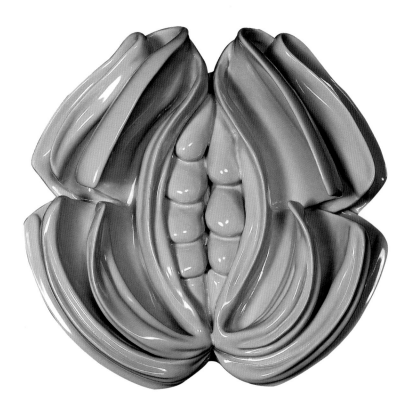

Virginia Woolf, TEST PLATE, 1978

Virginia Woolf, STUDY, 1978

RIGHT: *The Dinner Party* (detail), 1979, VIRGINIA WOOLF PLACE SETTING

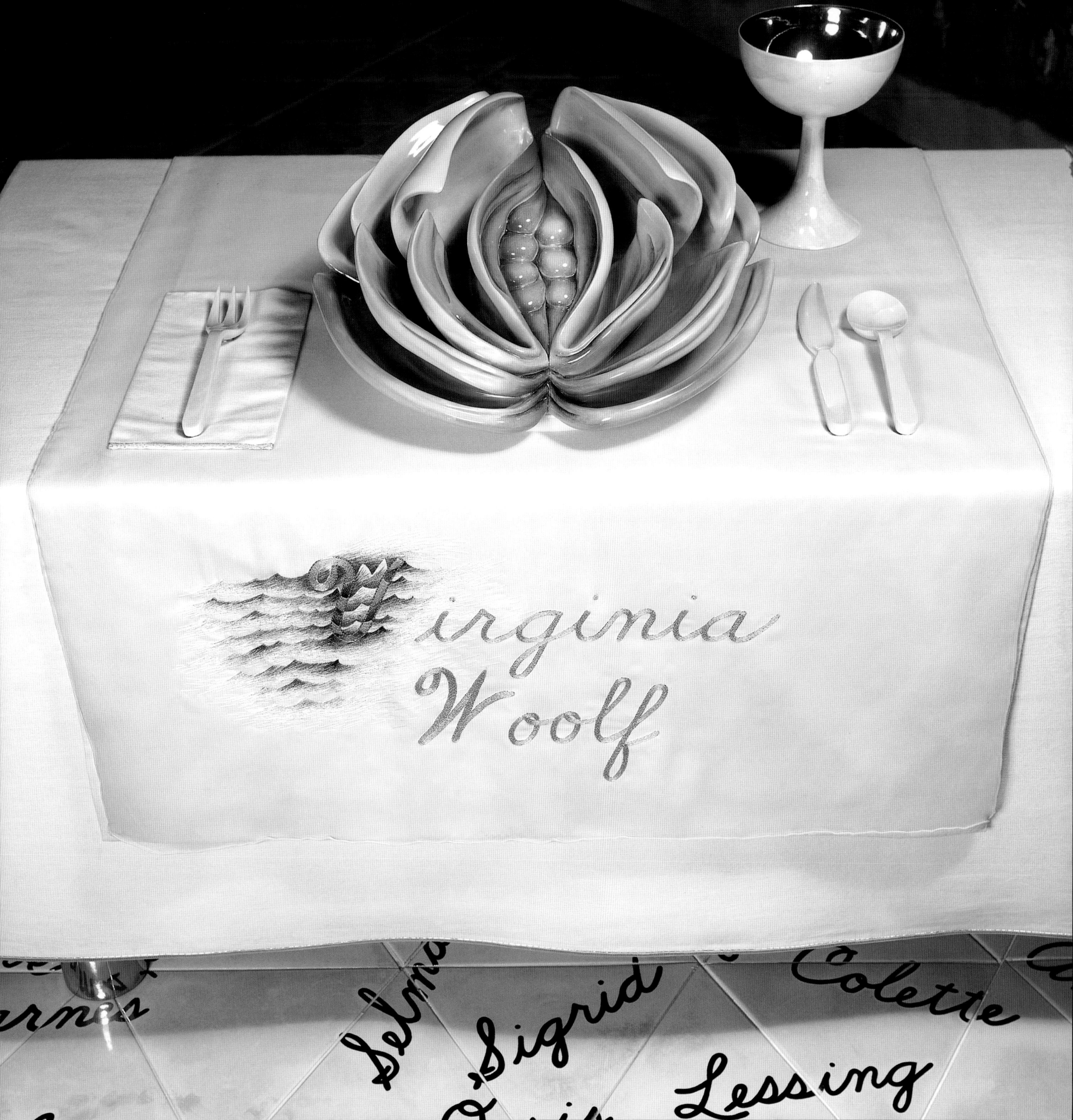
Virginia
Woolf
Colette
Sigrid
Lessing

THE BIRTH PROJECT YEARS

>>> 1980–1985

To my dismay, I discovered that there were too few images of birth in Western art, an omission I set out to counter through an extended series of painted and needleworked images of birth. To behold the vulva in labor as a woman is giving birth is to be confronted with sheer female power. I wanted to celebrate that power and to explore and express the range of birth experiences—the painful and the joyous—and the act of creation itself.

The Crowning, 1981

69

Then out of the chaos there emerged a sigh
And this sigh became a moon
And this moon became a wail
And this wail became a scream of birth

The screams of its birth
sent forth circles of sound into the darkness
And these circles of sound whirled through the void
forming a great shape
And this was the shape of the Universe

And then
with a great burst of light
The Universe reached the

In the beginning there was nothing for all was dark and chaotic   And mighty was this birth for it was the birth of the Universe   And out of this

In the Beginning, 1982

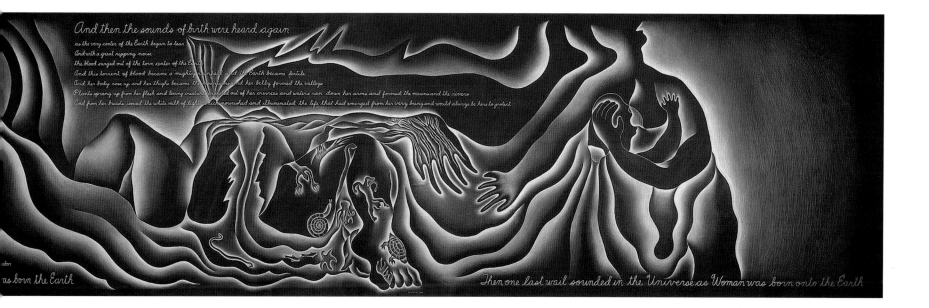

And then the sounds of birth were heard again
as the very center of the Earth began to tear
And with a great ripping noise
the blood surged out of the torn center of the Earth
And this torrent of blood became a mighty rainfall until the Earth became fertile
And her body rose up and her thighs became the mountains and her belly formed the valleys
Plants sprang up from her flesh and living creatures crawled out of her crevices and waters ran down her arms and formed the oceans and the rivers
And from her breasts issued the white milk of light which nourished and illuminated the life that had emerged from her very being and would always be hers to protect

...as born the Earth

Then one last wail sounded in the Universe as Woman was born onto the Earth

Birth Drawing, 1981

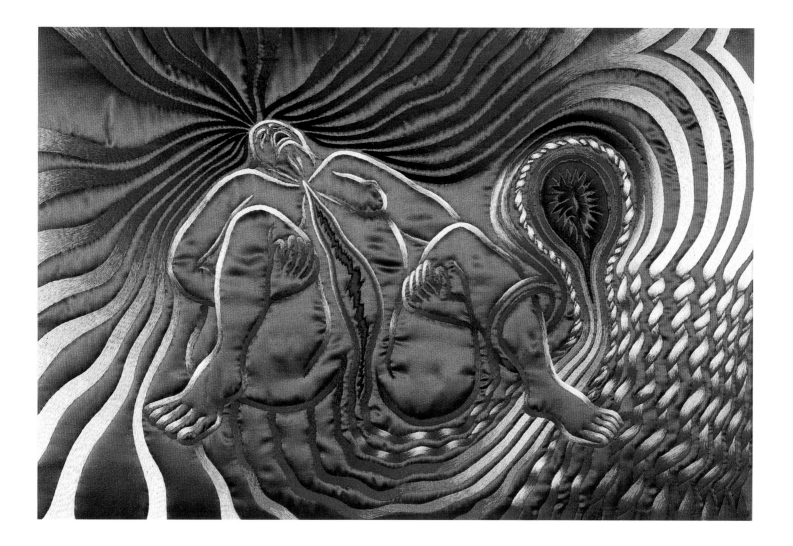

Birth Tear, 1982

Birth Trinity, 1983

The Creation, 1984

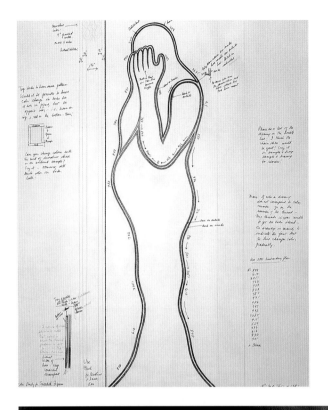

Drawing for *Smocked Figure*, 1984   Installation for *Smocked Figure*, 1984

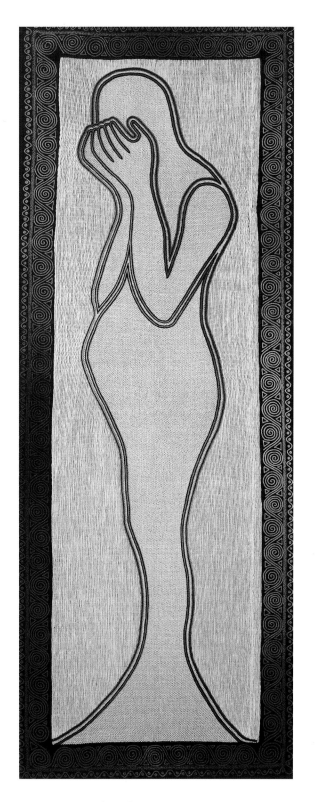

Smocked Figure (detail), 1984

THE POWERPLAY SERIES

>>> 1983–1987

For four years, I explored the gender construct of masculinity and its effects on male personalities and the world. Eventually I decided to create imagery about a new masculine ideal, one in which strength and vulnerability were merged.

Woe/Man, 1986

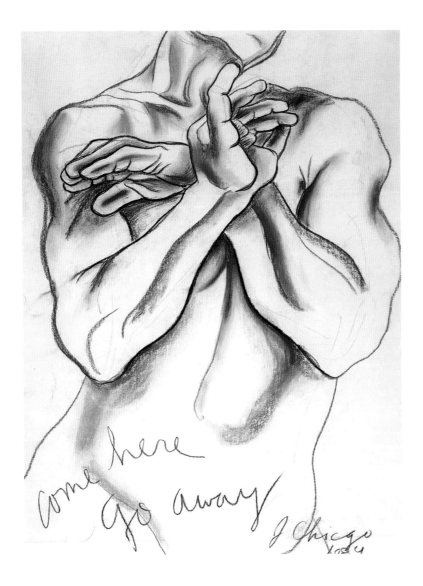

Come Here/Go Away, 1984

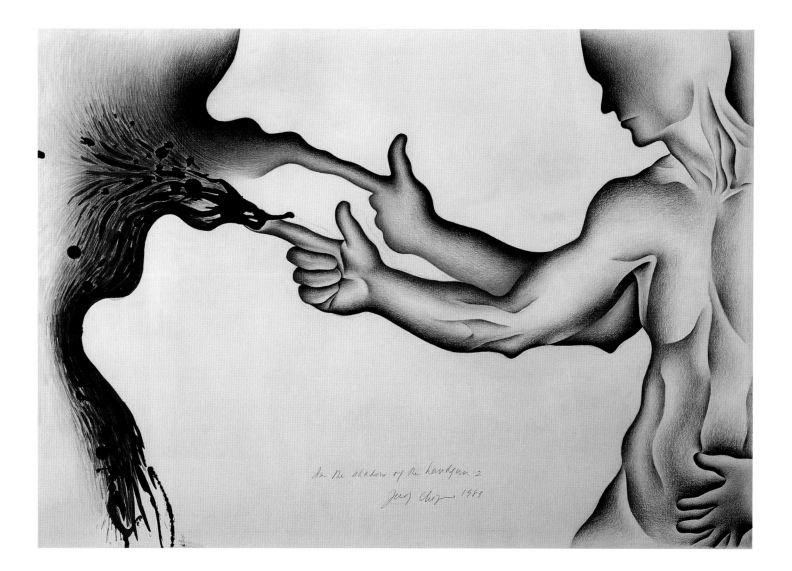

STUDY 2 FOR *In the Shadow of the Handgun*, 1983

81

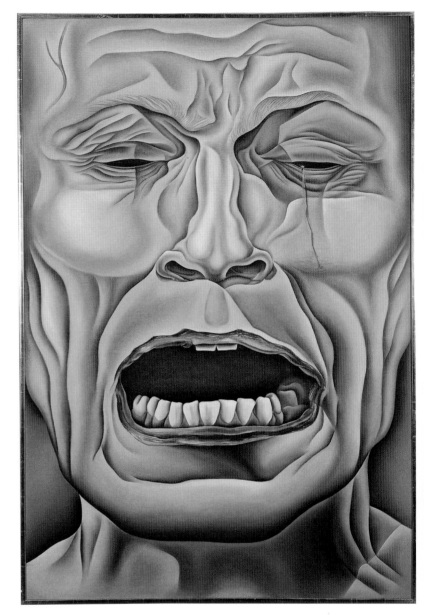

Three Faces of Man, 1985

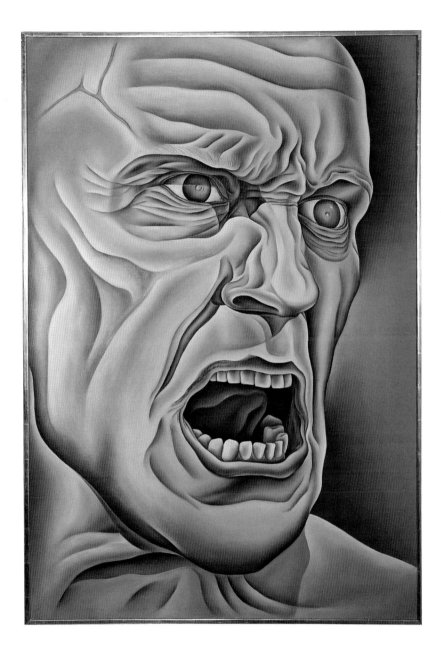

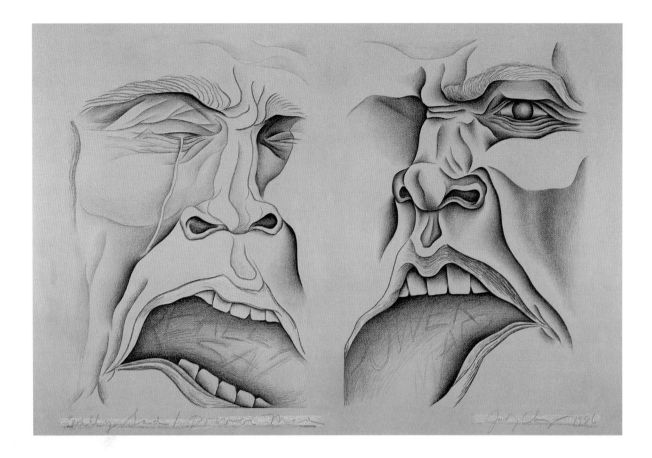

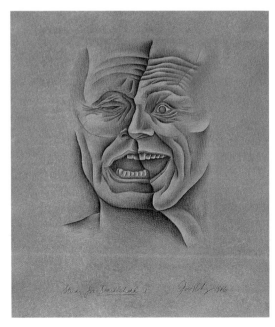

TOP: *Really Sad/Power Mad*, 1986

STUDY FOR *Doublehead I*, 1986

Lavender Doublehead/Hold Me, 1986

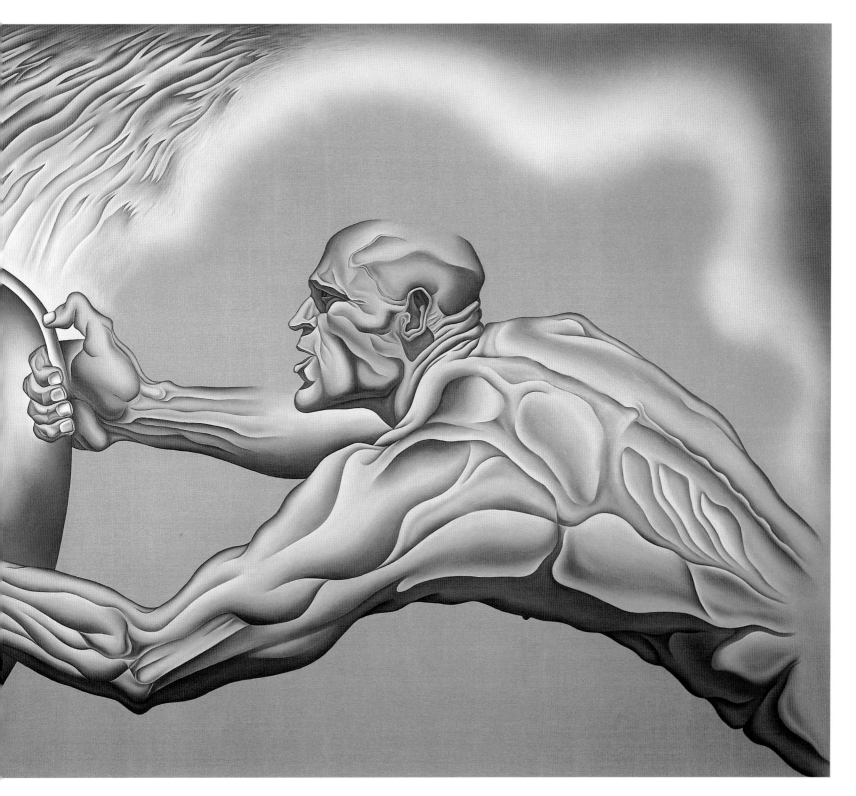

Driving the World to Destruction, 1985

THE HOLOCAUST PROJECT YEARS

>>> 1985–1993

Eight years in the making, the Holocaust Project was the most challenging project I ever undertook. Together with my husband, photographer Donald Woodman, I made an arduous journey into the darkness of the Holocaust, eventually locating its roots in a larger global structure of oppression and injustice, a structure that—many years after the Holocaust—continues to dominate and disfigure our planet.

Holocaust Project Logo, 1992

The Fall, 1993

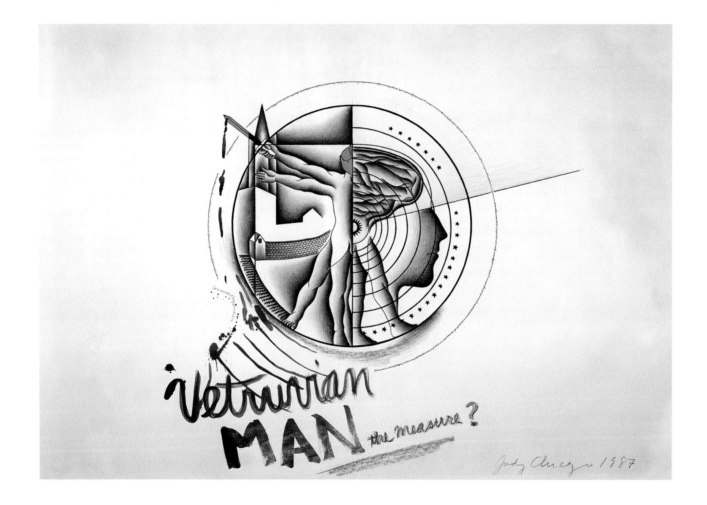

Vetruvian Man, the Measure?, 1987

Stairway to Death, 1989

What Would You Have Done?, 1989

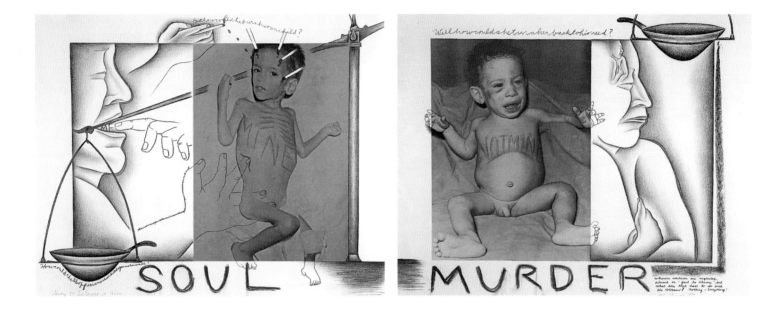

Soul Murder, STUDY FOR *Im/Balance of Power,* 1991

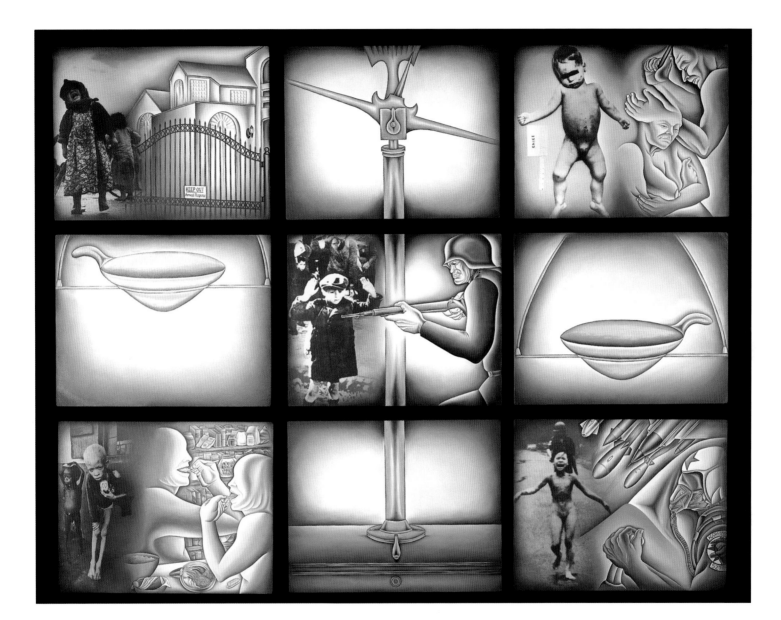

Im/Balance of Power, 1989

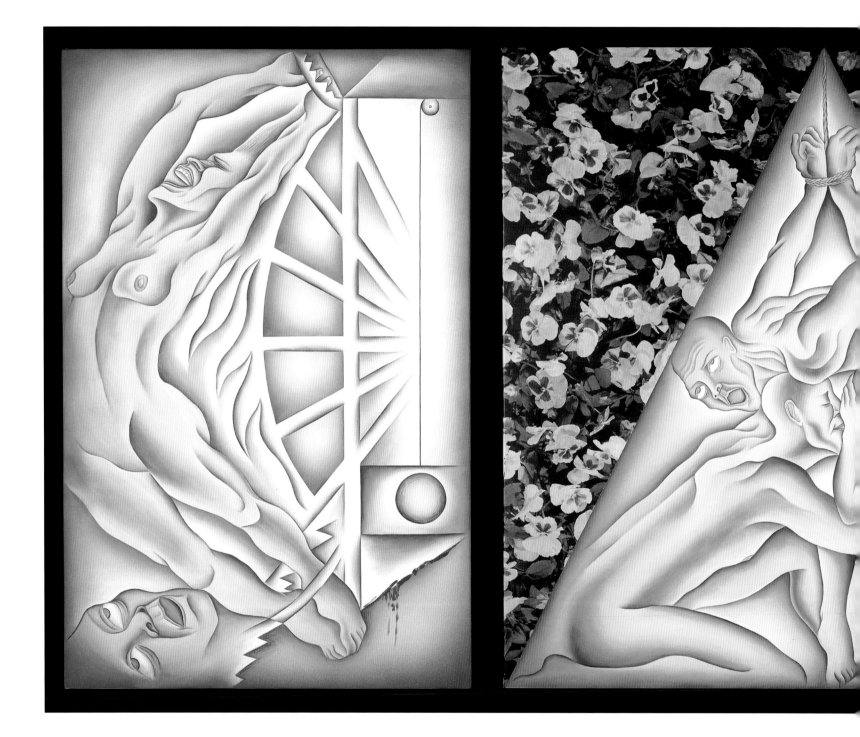

Pink Triangle/Torture, 1988

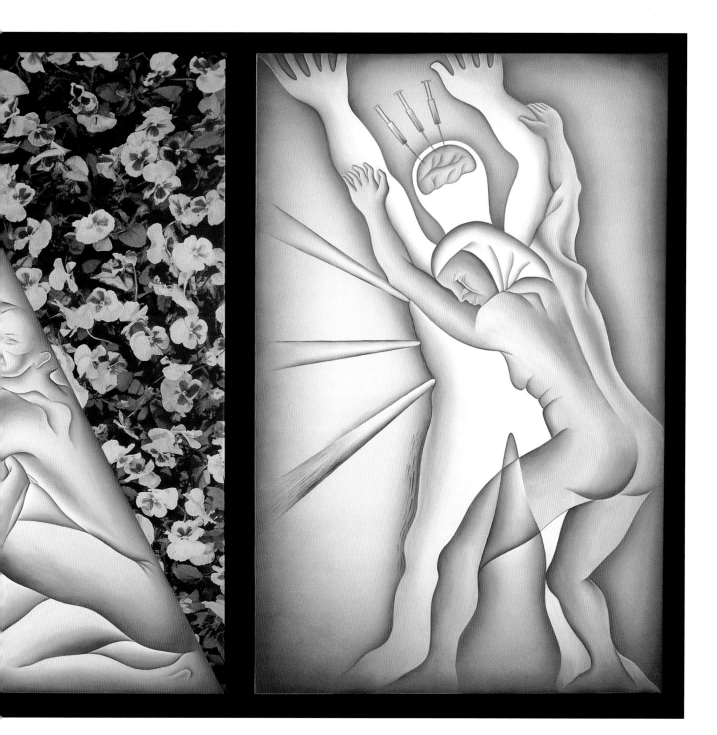

Pansy Crucifixion, 1988

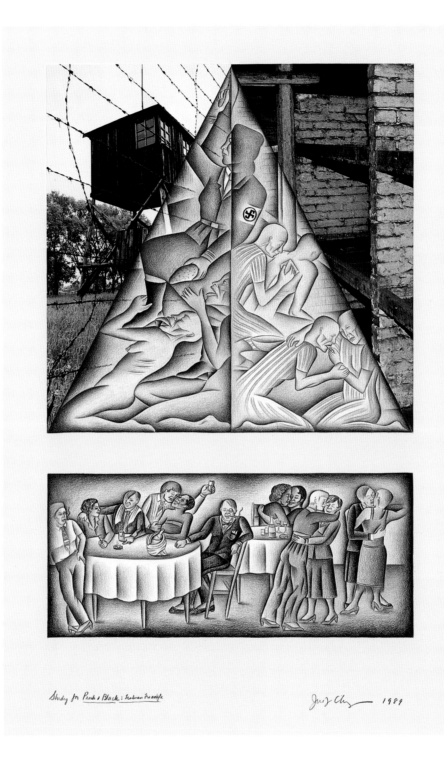

Study for Pink & Black: Lesbian Triangle   Judy Chicago 1989

FINAL STUDY FOR *Lesbian Triangle*, 1989

Arbeit Macht Frei/Work Makes Who Free?, 1992

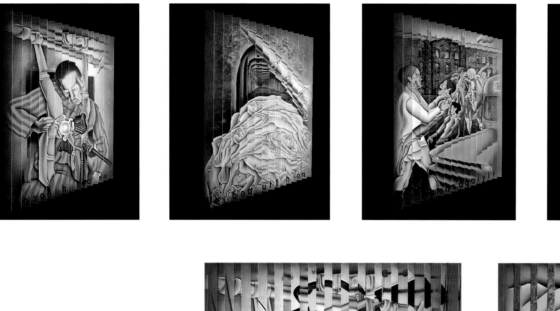

Four Questions, VIEW FROM LEFT, FRONTAL VIEW, VIEW FROM RIGHT, 1993

Rainbow Shabbat, 1992

107

THE END OF THE CENTURY
>>> 1993–2000

My outlook toward the world was greatly changed during the years I spent immersed in the subject of the Holocaust. Although tempted to succumb to despair in the face of what I had learned, I instead followed the Talmudic injunction to "choose life," which led me to my most recent project, *Resolutions: A Stitch in Time*. As always, I continued to produce individual works—some intensely personal, others exploring new aspects of women's experience and the ideal of mutual desire.

Find It in Your Heart, FROM *Resolutions: A Stitch in Time*, 2000

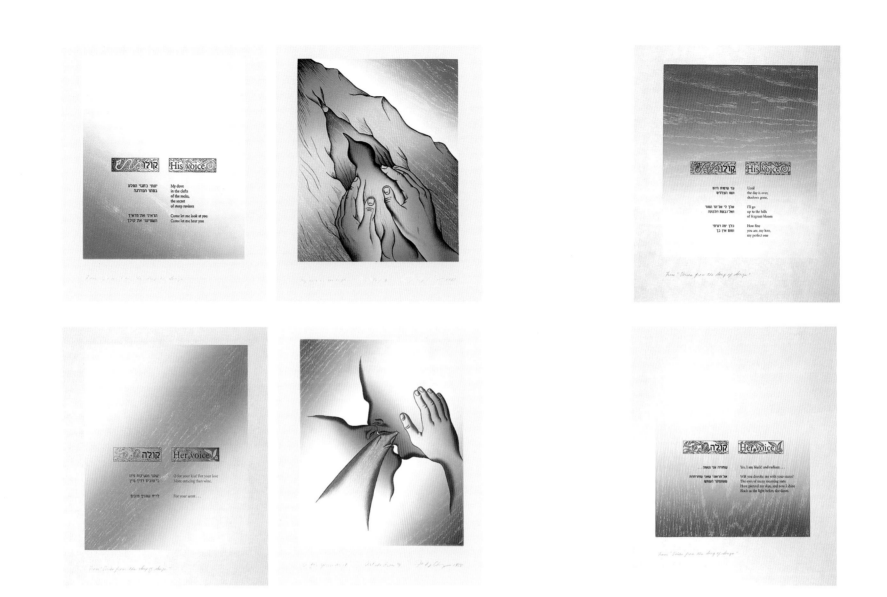

TOP: *My dove in the clefts of the rock*, FROM *Voices from the Song of Songs*, 1998–2000
BOTTOM: *O For your scent*, FROM *Voices from the Song of Songs*, 1998–2000

TOP: *How fine you are, my love*, FROM *Voices from the Song of Songs*, 1998–2000

BOTTOM: *Yes, I am black and radiant*, FROM *Voices from the Song of Songs*, 1998–2000

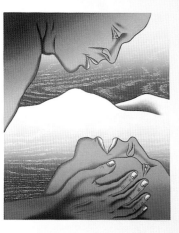

TOP: *There you stand like a palm*, FROM *Voices from the Song of Songs*, 1998-2000

BOTTOM: *Come, let us go out to the open fields*, FROM *Voices from the Song of Songs*, 1998-2000

LEFT: *Arcanum in Shades of Gray*, 2000
RIGHT: *Peeling Back* (AFTER *Female Rejection Drawing #3*), 2000

INSTALLATION FOR *Autobiography of a Year: June 1993 to November 1994*

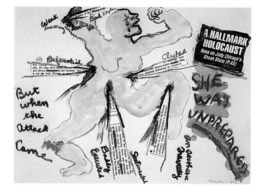

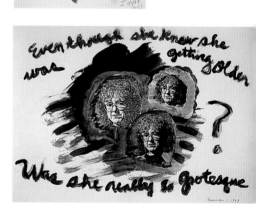

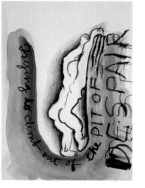

Autobiography of a Year (detail)

JUDY CHICAGO
>>> THE COURAGE OF SINGULAR CONVICTION

INTRODUCTION: FEMINIST PRESENCE

"My success is fragile, as fragile as the success of the women who preceded me. I've always looked at art in terms of the long, old, big historic picture. I know when I went to art school I was told there were never any great women artists. History has been repeatedly erased and as a result women have a great deal of difficulty being able to build on their predecessors rather than reinventing the wheel. My work embodies and insists upon a reclamation of women's history, for males and females, because to have the history of men is to have only half of human history." –JC[1]

Whether her work addresses identity or issues like the Holocaust, Judy Chicago never wavers from a feminist perspective. Judy Chicago's work keeps a question hovering: What does it mean to be a female person who is an artist? In a culture that still heavily favors the male artist, this question is essential.

Judy Chicago is fueled in part by the lack of a complete female historical record. Eager and aspiring, but rightly afraid her work would be erased, Chicago wanted to provide the historical record and the educational vehicles for a public unused to artwork from a definite female point of view and therefore tackled the added duties of historian, critic, and esthetician. She is the author of seven books and the coauthor of one.[2] Her books and lectures often provide documentation, context, and interpretation of the work she produced as an artist. It is noteworthy that critic and writer Lucy Lippard readily accepted Chicago's self-interpretation of the meaning for the predominant *Dinner Party* plate symbols, a merging of the butterfly and vagina images, for her 1980 article on the piece for *Art in America*.[3] Judy Chicago pioneered Feminist Art—she coined the phrase itself.

In 1964 Chicago graduated from UCLA with a Masters in Painting and Sculpture. Works like the 1964 *Mother Superette*, with their organic hints of subject matter to come, had been harshly ridiculed by Chicago's male professors.[4] It was, in part, the result of her negative experiences in graduate school that led her, at the end of the sixties, to mine the eroded and inconsistent veins of women's history. An early visual result was the *Great Ladies* series (1972–1973). In 1970 she began the first Feminist Art Program at California State University at Fresno and she also set her students to piecing together, as best they could, available material on women artists from contemporary and historical sources. Chicago's first autobiography, *Through the Flower: My Struggle as a Woman Artist*, includes a chapter utilizing Chicago's own research on women's art history. Although recent statistics on women artists point to the need for continuing reform,[5] it is through the efforts of pioneering artists like Chicago that an appropriate context is growing for the viewing, understanding, and judging of artwork by women.

THE FEMINIST ART PROGRAMS

I put my focus on younger women's education, so they wouldn't have to go through what I went through— to waste ten years running away from their impulses as women because they felt ashamed or because they felt like something was wrong with them because they were women. I wanted them to know they had a history they could be proud of. I didn't want them to go through a dis-identifying process. I wanted to change things for myself and I wanted to change things for other women. –JC

The founding of the first Feminist Art Program in the United States at Fresno State and then with Miriam Schapiro at the California Institute of the Arts in Valencia alone would have been enough to place Chicago within the history of postmodernism as well as the nexus of Feminist Art. At CalArts the Program created the groundbreaking *Womanhouse*, a collaborative student-and-instructor–produced installation and performance piece encompassing an actual house. Whether subsequent feminist artists, critics, or theorists professed to hail these founding feminist efforts, or to criticize them, the issues put forward by this program and its work became the agenda that was used for further exploration and development in the feminist community.

Chicago's experiences with the Feminist Art Program helped to change her and her art production. The hints at female identity and point of view found in pieces like the formalist and highly abstracted *Doorway* images gave way to overt declaration in pieces like the Prismacolor series *Rejection Quintet*. Although the agenda established in the Feminist Program demonstrated a daring, spirited attitude, this agenda was developed in a supportive all-female environment. Chicago's works made apart from the program required the courage of singular conviction. Chicago identifies *Female Rejection Drawing #3 (Peeling Back)* (1974) as her first two-dimensional work in which form and content completely meshed.[6] Chicago drew the abstracted petaled forms, which had appeared in her previous work, as peeling or bending back, one by one, to reveal the truth of her subject matter, her own femaleness, as represented by an unmistakable and centralized vaginal image. Chicago saw this "breakthrough" more as a return to the natural inclinations that emerged and then were suppressed in graduate school.

COLLABORATION AND DOCUMENTATION

I acknowledged what they [the women and men who worked on various Chicago projects] had contributed as a way of saying the world would be a better place if everybody's contributions were recognized. I wanted to strengthen the understanding that each person has something to offer and that every human experience has validity. —JC

The Feminist Art Program demonstrated how the group structure not only inspired a more profound imagery, but provided a context for acceptance. Although the concept and major design work of Chicago's next comprehensive venture, *The Dinner Party* (1979), can only be credited to the artist herself, the piece was nonetheless born of collaboration[7] and benefited from the process. Approximately four hundred people (women and a few men) worked on *The Dinner Party* during the five years of its production. Chicago reveals in an interview with Norma Broude and Mary Garrard for their book, *The Power of Feminist Art*, that her first plate designs unsettled her. "I felt terrified by the images that were coming out." Chicago goes on to say, "It wasn't really until I had the support of the community I built in *The Dinner Party* studio that I broke through this. I would make a drawing that, had I been by myself, I would have censored. But everybody said, 'Oh my God, that's fabulous!' . . . I began to accept my natural impulses which had been in all my early work."[8]

The two *The Dinner Party* volumes—*The Dinner Party: A Symbol of Our Heritage*, published in 1979 concurrently with the inaugural exhibition of the piece, and *Embroidering Our Heritage: The Dinner Party Needlework*, published the following year—tell the story of the collaborative birth of this iconic work. This history of select women in Western civilization, in visual and textual form, *The Dinner Party* consists of myriad components. Entrance banners and documentation accompany each exhibition of the work. A triangular table, forty-eight feet per side, is arranged with thirty-nine commemorative settings in which sculptural ceramic plate forms, with napkins, knives, forks, spoons, and goblets, sit on individualized needleworked tablecloth runners. Each plate setting creates a memorial to the life of an individual woman in history. The whole is complemented by the additional 999 names of women penned across the 2,300 lustrous triangular tiles that comprise the raised floor on which the table sits. *The Dinner Party* thus images a collaboration that is a collective or combined history of 1,038 women, through a process that was itself collaborative.

The collaborators assisted in compiling historical research as well as producing the physical components of the whole, including some elements of design within sections of the work. In *The Dinner Party* documentation Ann Isolde describes her interaction with Chicago on one of the preliminary drawings for the banners slated to hang at the entranceway to each exhibition of the table: "I hesitated at first, and then I knew I had to get right down there on the paper too. I got the pencil, the markers, the eraser and went into the drawing with her. It was incredible!"[9]

In keeping with the egalitarian spirit evoked by the Feminist Art Program, and in contrast to the long-standing tradition whereby artists do not publicly acknowledge their collaborators,[10] Chicago credited those who worked on the project, listing their names at each exhibition as well as in the accompanying documentary books. Even various individual collaborator's comments, such as the Isolde memory, are integrated into the text of those books.

Although Chicago freely wrote of her struggle with the collaborative process, she continued to work in that mode for three other projects, the *Birth Project*, the *Holocaust Project*, and *Resolutions: A Stitch in Time*. The *Birth Project*, which honors mythological, spiritual, and actual aspects of the birthing female, features the skills of 150 needleworkers in a series of 84 exhibition units and represents a zenith in Chicago's collaborative endeavors. Once again the concept was Chicago's, as were the primary designs, but the give and take among needleworkers and Chicago, and anyone else involved, provides an important ingredient toward understanding the work. A look at *Smocked Figure* is demonstrative. Chicago began with a Prismacolor and graphite drawing on paper. Mary Ewanoski, a needleworker from Goleta, California, then translated the drawing into a smocked and embroidered textile. The final exhibition featured documentation panels explaining the process, which (in this instance) include comments by Chicago and Ewanoski. Ewanoski's words provide a brief primer on the stitchery necessary, an examination of her interaction with Chicago, and her own interpretation of the meaning of the work. Therefore the artwork is not limited to the textile or the drawing but is a combination of the elements of what came to be called the *Birth Project* exhibition unit: the finished drawing, the finished textile, and documentation of the collaborative process.

THE RELATIONSHIP TO A BROAD AUDIENCE

We have cut art off from the larger human experience and have rendered it inaccessible to all but a few. I feel strongly about wanting to make a contribution to an expanded role for art because I feel we've lost contact with why art is important.
I believe it's a very hard thing to be authentic to human experience. You have to use your compassion, your intellect, your understanding, your emotions, your empathy, your talent, your insights, and your sensitivity to understand. —JC

By 1976 *ARTnews* reported that Chicago condemned elitism and quoted her as saying, "I want art again to be connected to human value and meaning."[11] Those sentiments for Chicago meant a return to authentic content, the content of her own experiences and the lives of other women, historic and contemporary. In 1985 she spoke about the *Birth Project* "extend[ing] the democratization of art begun by *The Dinner Party*."[12] By 1993 and the publication of the *Holocaust Project* book, Chicago's sense of authentic experience had expanded into an exploration of her own Jewish heritage and, by extension, the lives of other Jews.

Chicago's books about the *The Dinner Party*, the *Birth Project*, and the *Holocaust Project* forward her goal of creating an art both related to, and accessible to, a broad audience. Although Chicago may view the texts as entirely separate from the objects created, the documentation of each affects the meaning of each. With the *Holocaust Project* the meaning is affected by knowing that Chicago and collaborator/husband Donald Woodman saw an aspect of their work as an exploration of their own heritage. They immersed themselves in a study of the tragedy; they visited European Holocaust sites and reacted viscerally. This exploration modified their thinking, which led to a new attitude toward the Holocaust and the decision to utilize combines, a blending of painting and photography.[13]

The Dinner Party book is helpful for a full understanding of the work. In the truest sense, *The Dinner Party* is about documentation—about examining and honoring experience and giving credit. Multiple histories are recorded and credited through *The Dinner Party*—those of the women commemorated with their names at the table and those of the women (and men) who put them there. It is through Chicago's documentation of this heroic collaboration that heroic acts can be seen for the contextual events they are, and allows the acts of the women commemorated at the table to become more real. This documentation also provides a way for individual women to look with empathy and to identify, to see themselves as meaningful collaborators within the historical enterprise, even to see themselves as taking a rightful place at the table of history without regard to the size or type of each one's contribution.

For the *Birth Project*, because the units were not originally intended to be exhibited as a whole, it is only through the book that Chicago's overall concept becomes known. The book unifies the story of the process and much of the imagery into a spatial and cognitive proximity and therefore it assumes a pivotal role. The book illustrates how each textile (with its various societally identified female technique) relies on its interaction with other textiles and provides for an accumulation of their meanings. Without a comprehensive exhibition of the *Birth Project* pieces, the book is also necessary for a complete view of the collaborators and the means of the *Birth Project*'s accomplishment. The collaboration of the work's making is as much its subject as is "birth" in its metaphoric role for creativity.

The story of the making of the *Birth Project* itself provides the suggestion of proof of its own meaning: female sexuality can provide an alternate psychic energy for any creation. As Carol Duncan pointed out in "Virility and Domination in Early Twentieth-Century Vanguard Painting," male artists have sometimes overtly identified their sexuality as an energizing source for their work. Duncan uses Maurice de Vlaminck's remarks to clarify her observation. "Vlaminck, although primarily a landscape painter, could still identify his paintbrush with his penis: 'I try to paint with my heart and my loins, not bothering with style.'"[14]

For both *The Dinner Party* and the *Birth Project*, the meaning of their making assumes a place of importance along with the things made. The documentation of both works exists in the tradition of a twentieth-century innovation, one from the 1960s in which art is viewed as concept and all is accepted that furthers or strengthens that concept. In essence, anyone who owns *The Dinner Party* books (the 1979 or 1980 publications) or the *Birth Project* volume has immediate, although partial, access to the art-making process.

Unlike preceding artists who explored the topic of the Holocaust, Chicago looked, as she wrote in the book that accompanied the *Holocaust Project*, for "the connection of the Holocaust with other historical events."[15] The project includes imagery about sexism, child abuse, nuclear and military proliferation, homophobia, the genocide of native peoples, slavery, the inequity of wealth distribution, cruelty to animals, the use of knowledge as power by the medical and science establishments, and environmental rape. For example, the imagery for *The Fall* and *Im/Balance of Power* directly emphasizes this systemic approach, while pieces like *Pink Triangle/Torture* narrow the focus to concentrate on more singular atrocities—in this case the persecution of homosexuals by the Nazis. Placed within a compact triangular arrangement, the imagery of abuse nevertheless provides a segue into a selected history of politically motivated torture. Placed on a panel to the left of the centrally situated and tortured homosexual men is a woman/witch stretched on a medieval rack flanked by a severed head on one side and a French guillotine on the other. Placed on a panel to the right of the center section is an allusion to more current types of torture, like that practiced by the Chilean dictator Augusto Pinochet, with his predilection for "disappearing" selected "foes" of his regime. Thus Chicago evokes, in very specific terms, the relationship of the Holocaust to us all, no matter our gender, our race, our religion, our sexual preference, or our culture.

HISTORICAL ROOTS

One of the consequences of my struggle has been a sense of shame, about my own empowerment and my directness. The only way I could handle it was to transform my impulses into a perfect finish, a perfect image, totally controlled.
I'm this vulnerable person who feels really deeply and who expresses her every emotion, and I'm this person who thinks really deeply about issues and both sides of me appear in my art. When it comes together, when there is a meshing of thinking and feeling, that I think is the best art. —JC

By the early 1970s, as a product of forms like Conceptual or Performance Art, documentation had entered the acceptable contemporary canon, but much of the visual language utilized by Chicago at various points during her career had not. From the Feminist Art Program Chicago herself had taken on the controversial agenda and imagery as expressed in the fomentation of the Program's processes and production. But Chicago also utilized, knowingly or subconsciously, influences from contemporary art. Her modernist roots, in the form of a mesh of 1960s influences, are evident in works from *The Dinner Party* to the more recent *Holocaust Project*. Her use of photographs, preparatory materials, text, repetition, soft media, subject matter, social comment, and the integration of art and life could be considered vestigial aspects of previous developments in Conceptual and Process Art, Happenings, and Pop Art. However, these vestiges are all transformed by an earnest rather than a jaded attitude. The ideas she adopted were substantive. Her process included a comprehensiveness in which attention is given to every detail as well as the work's final presentation.

Laura Meyer has shown the direct influence on *The Dinner Party* of the 1960s California Finish Fetish movement, a movement dedicated to minimal form, luminous surface effects, emphasis on technical bravado, and the suppression of evidence of the intense labor used to achieve end results. All Chicago's other major projects, as they have been exhibited—although internal processes, media, and subject matter may change—share several of the southern California movement's characteristics: a devotion to "technical precision," whatever the technique, and a flawless sense of "finish." But Meyer goes on to comment on the way in which *The Dinner Party* opposed the tenets and meaning of the movement:

> Studied at close range, the work contains a plethora of curving, folded, layered surfaces, an array of contrasting colors and textures. While the Los Angeles "cool school" attempted to eliminate all evidence of human touch from its work, *The Dinner Party* displays the signs of its laborious creation like a badge of sainthood. If Finish Fetish was. . . amoral, *The Dinner Party* is a profoundly moralizing work of art.[16]

All Chicago's works (after her early modernist/formalist period) share these oppositional aspects: a sense of complexity (even when surfaces appear streamlined or simplified), the lure of the "human touch," and a "moralizing" approach.

The dual impulse toward precision and finish are evident even in some of Chicago's preparatory drawings, for example works like the color drawing for *The Dinner Party* runner, *Eleanor of Aquitaine*. In the *Eleanor* work Chicago concentrates on a full rendering of plant material and merely suggests, with a faint outline, a bordering fence. However, the *Eleanor* drawing still presents a smooth surface finish and conveys a sense of precision. Its suggestive passages and Chicago's penciled remarks appear planned. Its contrasting passages of filled and unfilled space, and the remarks, occupy the strategic placement of a contemplated compositional balance. The Finish Fetish legacy can be applied to other preparatory pieces like the final studies for the *Holocaust Project*. These taut drawings, though precursory, convey a sense that every aspect of the work must be controlled. From the details of the imagery to the way the media is applied to the surface of the paper, the work is constructed so that any idiosyncratic move of the hand, thoughtless gesture, or oversight is eliminated.

Nevertheless, Chicago has produced a prodigious quantity of imagery on paper that is in seeming contrast to the quest for a "perfected" outcome. She has produced scratchy, crude, spontaneous, or assuredly quick work that matches lightning thought or indignation, or other feelings, to the gestural movement of the hand. Often these pieces exist as autobiographical work or as early sketches in the process of thinking through the subject matter or concept at hand. However, even many of these "unperfected" images convey a sense of completeness. For example, in the *Holocaust* study titled *Pansies, Is That a Reason?* the scrawl of the hand is matched by the scream in the question. Generally this imagery reveals the side of the artist that is fast to think, to speak, to challenge, to risk, to show vulnerability, and to be "direct"—as Chicago characterizes this trait herself.

POSTMODERN ISSUES

Why is oil paint on canvas inherently better than china paint on porcelain? Because somebody said so and because that somebody had power to enforce what he thought. I try to pick media appropriate to my intent or my content. So, I don't care if it is high or low, male or female. Most people think in a hierarchical structure. If you move out of that, there is another way of thinking—a different way of treating media, people, and other species—and an alternative way of evaluating art. As long as you stand inside the hierarchical structure, you can't begin to imagine another way of living, seeing, evaluating, or being. Feminist thinking has expanded tremendously, making links in terms of race, class, ethnicity, and so on. —JC

Before the term had been defined or disseminated, Chicago's work—in postmodern fashion—began to cross boundaries into other fields such as theology, history, or psychology. Feminist theologians like Carol Christ or Naomi Goldenberg mentioned Chicago and her imagery in their early groundbreaking writings as the potential creator of visual symbols for a developing or evolving faith within Western society. A cursory glance at other characteristics, as delineated by Charles Jencks, an early theorist of the postmodern, quickly shows this alignment of Chicago's work with what became modernism's replacement.

Chicago's work relates to the lives of people in broad, but ironically specific, audiences (for instance, the women's movement community or the Jewish community) and her works are generally nonhierarchical in attitude. In *The Dinner Party*, for example, every place setting is given equal visual weight. Although this configuration may appear formalist, Chicago's motivations were not. In the *Holocaust Project* that leveling continues. The Jewish experience is viewed as distinctive, but so is the suffering of others (examples include aboriginal peoples or African Americans or homosexuals and lesbians).

Chicago's works have revived historical media (like needlework and micrography) and images (like preindustrial images of women giving birth or archived photographs of the Holocaust). Chicago works to capture a simultaneous sense of the new with the old, as in *The Dinner Party* with its contemporary mixed media approach to the use of traditional ceramics and needlework, both of which carry millennia of history behind them. In addition, her craft media, hierarchically seen as "minor" or "low" by the art establishment, is transformed by its treatment into a "fine" or "high" category, thus challenging the existence of such categories. A similar conclusion can be drawn from Chicago's combined use of photography and painting in the *Holocaust Project*. Photography is often viewed as a modern technology, while painting is seen as a venerable, higher art form. The conflation of old and new media, or high and low media, in a nonhierarchical treatment has become a hallmark of Chicago's oeuvre.

Chicago has also utilized a simultaneous elite/popular dichotomy. For example, she meant the *Birth Project* textiles as fine art (needleworked paintings),[17] but she prepared the work to be shown easily in populist spaces like libraries or hospitals. Her earlier work has clearly been critical of Western values through a flattening or broadening of the elitist divisions and categories of the art world, but particularly through a general criticism of the lopsided distribution of power that disenfranchises groups socially constructed by gender, race, religion, and other designations. Chicago's collaborative process challenges the notion of elitism in which a pinnacle can be achieved by one person alone. Instead, her collaborative working processes expose the notion of the "top" as simply a positioned denial of the supportive or collaborative network. Chicago has worked to avoid a dishonest view whereby the collaborative network is unacknowledged. Chicago's inclusive approach not only extends toward alternative processes but toward an evocative relationship to a large public audience.

Although writers differ in their various and evolved definitions of the postmodern, more recent critics have frequently referred to the overlapping "universalizing" and "essentializing" tendencies of Chicago's work. Considered a double heresy, the first tendency is viewed as nonpostmodern and the second is seen as an unenlightened form of feminist thinking. In the Chicago interview for *The Power of Feminist Art*, Broude and Garrard broached these topics. Chicago countered the "universalizing" charge by saying that her work "articulat[ed]. . . an enlarged dialogue about art, with new and more diverse participants,"[18] a means to engaging and empowering the many individual voices within the community. Over the course of the forty years of her career, Chicago utilized a number of methods to effect her intentions. Besides sharing her art-making with others (professional artists and nonprofessionals), she operated from a definitely stated point of view, and connected, more than universalized, her own issues with those of other individuals and groups. So, in *The Dinner Party* she connected the distinct lives of women across time, or in the *Holocaust Project* she connected disparate peoples and the historical events that disempowered them. In the *Smocked Figure* exhibition unit for the *Birth Project* she connected her process and intent with that of another woman. Significantly, here, it is the needleworker, Mary Ewanoski, who is quoted to offer a meaning for the image.

As a pioneer venturing into different imagistic, technical, and conceptual territory, Chicago may have found it difficult to find matching language to describe the intent and processes of her thinking or to find language to describe her art. For example, in 1973, when Chicago and Miriam Schapiro published their article on female imagery, which seemed to further provoke the first round of heated controversy they had begun within Feminist Art circles,[19] they did use the word "universal" in connection with the imagery they were describing. However, in attempting to show that the imagery they discussed grew out of the experience of each woman artist, they also spoke about the difference in "cultural experience" and "education" for males and females. They talked about "some" women or "many" women, or of Georgia O'Keeffe "transcend[ing] womanliness," while also contradictorily referring to "woman" in a generic, universalizing sense.[20]

Chicago's and Schapiro's own problems with language can only be compounded by the interpretive and strategic problems of pioneering postmodernist or feminist critics and art historians. In the nearly thirty years since the publication of that article, Chicago has continued to evolve and refine her language to meet the challenge of postmodernist inquiries. However, like her interviewers, Chicago may occasionally take simultaneous positions on postmodernist/modernist issues,[21] such as the willingness to share in the art-making process and consciously share in the interpretation of meaning while still privileging her position. She continues to use the word "universal" within various contexts.

In the 1990s many in the art world expressed a "weariness" of art theory,[22] nonetheless Chicago's body of work does span the gamut of characteristics now defined as postmodern. The work is therefore not easily classified. She cannot fit comfortably into just a "neo" category, or a "public art" category, or an "art and craft" category, to utilize some of the headings listed in anthologies for discussing the various styles and forms now accepted.[23] Her work, for instance, can be expressive and conceptual at the same time. Chicago says she sees herself as integrating thinking and feeling. On the one hand, Chicago is listed as a pioneer in the 1995 book *Mapping the Terrain: New Genre Public Art* edited by Suzanne Lacy, while, on the other, all five of her major projects integrate art with various craft media: ceramics and textiles in *The Dinner Party*, needlework/textiles in the *Birth Project*, weaving and paper-casting in *Powerplay*, weaving, needlework, and stained glass in the *Holocaust Project*, and needlework and painting in *Resolutions*.

A REDEFINITION OF THE NUDE: WOMEN AS SUBJECTS

I am interested in re-visioning and offering alternative ways of being, seeing, and doing. —JC

The woman of *The Crowning* is nude. In 1956 Kenneth Clark deemed the nude an "art form invented by the Greeks in the fifth century [B.C.], just as opera is an art form invented in seventeenth-century Italy."[24] In 1972, as the women's movement came into full swing, John Berger published *Ways of Seeing* in which he interpreted, through a Marxist lens, the post-Renaissance female nude (females increasingly became the predominant figures so depicted) as a form of capitalist exploitation by male "spectator-owner[s]."[25] Shortly thereafter, art historians like Mary Garrard and Carol Duncan framed questions about visual art female nudity within a feminist context. By the mid-1980s, the Guerrilla Girls were popularizing such scholarly questions with a notorious poster that asked: "Do women have to be naked to get into the Met[ropolitan] Museum?"

From the point of view of feminist writers, the nude can be used by artists as a malleable form for ever-evolving meaning. As Garrard points out in "Artemisia and Susanna,"[26] in 1610 Artemisia Gentileschi defiantly painted Susanna with the Elders as the nude victim she was. Duncan writes in "Virility and Domination in Early Twentieth-Century Vanguard Painting"[27] that in 1906 Paula Modersohn-Becker subverted the prevalent expression of the genre by infusing her own nude self-portrait with a sense of self-respect. Whitney Chadwick in *Women, Art, and Society* analyzes the nude subject in the 1908 *Grandmother and Young Girl Stepping into the Bath* by Suzanne Valadon as placed in a woman-identified, no-nonsense, gangly position, one that might actually be experienced by a female climbing into a bathtub.[28] More recently Alice Neel's nudes of individualized friends and acquaintances show a search for the whole person, the integration of the physical and the psychological. In her 1980 nude self-portrait, painted at the age of eighty, she showed the wisdom and the gumption to paint herself candidly from an integrated mind/body stance.

Although disparate in time, technique, style, and meaning, these very selective examples of nudes by Gentileschi, Modersohn-Becker, Valadon, and Neel nevertheless delineate for women viewers a change in the female nude form from object to subject. Women can identify with the conveyed fear and anger, tentative self-respect, or knowledge of self, physical and mental, portrayed by the artists. As Joanna Frueh described in *The Power of Feminist Art*, feminism intensified an interest in "The Body Through Women's Eyes."[29] Chicago's female nudes exist within a growing redefinition of the female nude while also contributing new forms and new meanings. Exemplary *Birth Project* figures, like *Birth Trinity* convey a state of mind/mood/body emphasizing energized actualization, an attitude of realized self-power, a knowledge of the connection of the self with the environment in which the self exists.

In the *Birth Project*, Chicago's nudes tend toward massiveness. They are generally fully displayed and fully nude. They may be sprawled before the viewer and even be in pain as in *Birth Tear*, but they cannot be dominated. They give birth metaphorically to everything physical, intellectual, and spiritual. The *Birth Project* figures provide an interesting contrast to a perusal of nude imagery by "the great masters" where an often titillating quality is applied to a portrayal of youngish, vulnerably displayed women for the voyeuristic pleasure of the viewer. Even in an artwork example where the women are given mass and energy, the female figures generally do not show confidence or a sense of their own power. A painting by Rubens with just such figures, *The Rape of the Daughters of Leucippus*, dramatically epitomizes the traditional gender division between the powerful male and the disempowered female nude, the subject and the object.

In 1986 Josephine Withers reviewed the *Birth Project* for the *New Art Examiner*. Although she judged the work with mixed assessments, she was clear in her praise of Chicago's treatment of the nude:

> Vulva and hair, not to speak of distended pregnant bellies and drooping breasts, vanished from the canon a very long time ago, and only reappeared in the last fifteen years or so in the matter-of-fact images of the real-ist painters and in "feminist" art. . . . Chicago's birthing images . . . are heroic challenges to the traditions that

emasculate (note that there is no gender-appropriate word here) woman's generative power either by sanitizing or humiliating her.[30]

By skirting much of the "canon" referred to by Withers, and in a reminiscence of sacred female statuary found in European Neolithic[31] sites, Chicago creates an inclusive nude image in *The Crowning*, unusual in contemporary figures. The figure of *The Crowning* is female and male: She has breasts and a vagina as well as a penile form that extends between her breasts. She is animal and plant: The outline of her body is lepidopteran and she carries the suggestion of pistils and stamens. She is matter, form, cognizant energy, patterns and lines of light and dark. Her centralized and symmetrical placement, as well as the alternate glow of light and dark, lend her a sacred quality. This figure holds herself and watches herself. In *The Crowning*, Chicago clearly strived for a symbol embodying the honored, integrated, and self-empowered placement of the female within an ecumenical and connected view of life.

A FEMALE GAZE

How can we get hold of the ways difference is driving us? Can we handle difference in a healthy way? —JC

While Chicago finished the *Birth Project*, she began to turn a "female gaze" toward men.[32] Unlike the attitudinal stance taken in the traditional objectification of the female nude, Chicago painted the male nude in *Powerplay* in an attempt to understand the effects of a cross-referenced system of gender and power. As art historian Paula Harper notes in the catalog for *Powerplay*, Chicago wanted to translate an uncensored understanding into visual form. Harper let Chicago's words speak for themselves, "I realized that men depict women and women depict women—women are everybody's love (or hate) object. And I said to myself—women are not the problem."[33]

In the work *Driving the World to Destruction*, Chicago fashioned a torso of muscles and sinews, hardened and knotted into its own grotesque landscape. With a boldly aggressive expression and eyes focused fiercely on the global panorama ahead, this figure steers the world with a V-for-victory–emblazoned wheel while the earth's continental masses flame out of control. Here Chicago conceived her vision of the "male problem," the problem of the "burden" of too much power: "It would drive one mad, literally power mad."[34]

With remarks that seem to presuppose the *Holocaust Project*, Paula Harper identifies *Powerplay* within a category she calls "art with survival value." She surmises, "Chicago's art alerts us to the danger of remaining fixed in sexual roles that no longer work in the modern era. . . . So new adaptive behavior is called for: women can no longer allow and encourage men to behave as they have in the past. . . . Women's own survival and the survival of the race is at stake."[35]

In the painting *Three Faces of Man*, Chicago hones in on the psychological realm of the power problem. She painted the facial striations of skin-covered musculature distorted into overwrought rage, anguish, or aggression. Chicago, like Harper, identifies the *Powerplay* images as an attempt to break traditionally codependent relationships that help foster and sustain systematically extreme behavior:

> Because women have been trained to hold up false mirrors to men and because men are not honest with one another since they're in competition, there's nobody to show them what's happened to them, what they look like, what they've become. . . . They're not the enemy. I wanted to show them as human, but acting in ways that are intolerable.[36]

FORM AND MESSAGE: LONG-LASTING MOODS AND MOTIVATIONS

In terms of real change, it has to be global change or it will sweep away. If enough of us shared a different vision, then solutions would be found. Many people shared the vision of a spacecraft going to Mars and a little robot getting out and walking around and taking pictures, and so they solved the problems and found solutions. Until there is a shared vision, solutions cannot take place.

Powerplay and the *Holocaust Project* demonstrate clearly how, for Chicago, feminism has been a life stance, a way of looking at herself and then positioning herself in relationship to western societal systems of power and history—systems that variously affect women, men, and cultural groups.[37] Such works, along with undertakings like *The Dinner Party* and the *Birth Project*, not to mention the myriad of other series or individual pieces, were constructed by Chicago to promote change. Chicago's artwork presses an alternative worldview, through her own system of forms/symbols, into the visual repertoire of viewers. Theologians view symbols as the language of religion, a means for relatively quickly transferring an array of beliefs, values, and behaviors. Anthropologist Clifford Geertz says that symbols provoke "powerful, pervasive, and long-lasting moods and motivations" and that "symbol systems . . . both express the [cultural] climate and shape it."[38]

Over the course of Chicago's career her imagery has attracted hundreds of collaborators, in some instances for years, sometimes even when collaborators developed personal difficulties with her. Chicago's exhibitions often set attendance records for each institution in which her works are shown. Institutions showing *The Dinner Party* (from the inaugural exhibition in 1979 to the latest exhibition in 1996) report an average of 50,000 viewers per venue. When the work was shown at the Brooklyn Museum of Art in 1980 the Museum had to consider crowd control, installing a Ticketron.[39] Not only has Chicago's imagery attracted hundreds of collaborators, but one million viewers all over the world.

The religio/anthropological theory of deep, psychic influence may explain the almost pilgrimatic voyage by many to see Chicago's work or the kind of testimonial reactions often given by individual viewers. This influence can explain, in part, the polarized positions often expressed: from the negative reaction of a critic like Robert Hughes who believes that art cannot make a societal difference,[40] to the reaction of a viewer who says, "I felt my whole consciousness shift a frame."[41]

Chicago says it is in the void that she finds the challenge, the impetus for the manufacture of images and symbols that give life to aspects denied, forgotten, suppressed, or never named by contemporary society. She has accepted that challenge through a variety of means: founding of the first Feminist Art Program in the United States; the invention of symbols/forms to match social messages; the redefinition of female-associated forms; the crossing of interdisciplinary boundaries; the use of media and technique to match the message so that "new" and "old" as well as "high" and "low" are mixed into a nonhierarchical treatment; documenting her collaborative process; developing a relationship with a large public audience. Chicago has worked since the 1960s to honor female imagery, including perspectives on personal identity, on the nature of art, and on political issues. She has produced an art that functions socially. Judy Chicago's accomplishments earn her an historical place as a pioneer of postmodern art and as a founder of Feminist Art.

Viki D. Thompson Wylder
Tallahassee, Florida
1 August 2001

1. Quotations by the artist are placed at the introduction of each section of this essay. These quotations are taken from an interview with the artist by the author. Subsequent quotations within the text, unless otherwise specified, are taken from the same source. In general, this interview informs the essay. The interview was completed in three segments in 1997 to 1998 as preparation for the Judy Chicago retrospective titled *Trials and Tributes*. That exhibition opened at Florida State University in February 1999 and toured until February 2002. This essay is an abridged version from the catalogue for *Trials and Tributes*. Viki D. Thompson Wylder, "Judy Chicago: Trials and Tributes," *Judy Chicago: Trials and Tributes*, ed. Allys Palladino-Craig (Tallahassee, FL: Florida State University Museum of Fine Arts, Museum Press, 1999), 8–29.

2. The following is a list of the titles and publishers of books by Judy Chicago: *Through the Flower: My Struggle as a Woman Artist* (Garden City, New York: Doubleday, 1975); *Beyond the Flower: The Autobiography of a Feminist Artist* (New York: Viking Penguin, 1996); *The Dinner Party: A Symbol of Our Heritage* (Garden City, New York: Anchor Press/Doubleday, 1979); *Embroidering Our Heritage: The Dinner Party Needlework* (Garden City, New York: Anchor Press/Doubleday 1980); *The Dinner Party* (New York: Penguin, 1996); *The Birth Project* (Garden City, New York: Doubleday, 1985); *The Holocaust Project* (New York: Penguin, 1993). Judy Chicago is the coauthor, with Edward Lucie-Smith, of *Women and Art: Contested Territory* (New York: Watson-Guptill, 1999).

3. Lucy Lippard, "Judy Chicago's *Dinner Party*," *Art in America*, April 1980, 114–126.

4. Chicago, *Through the Flower*, 34.

5. For example, blind juried exhibitions "appear to have a gender ratio comparable to the ratio of work submitted and to the ratio of available professional artists" while invitational exhibitions "tend to produce very biased gender (and racial) ratios that do not reflect the ratio of available professional artists." As Eleanor Dickinson points out "Invited exhibitions are far more numerous than juried exhibitions." Eleanor Dickinson, *Statistics: Gender Discrimination in the Art Field* (San Francisco, CA: Eleanor Dickinson, 2001), 18, 26.

These statistics are also distributed by a number of organizations including the Artists Equity Association, the Women's Caucus for Art, the Coalition of Women's Art Organizations, and the California Lawyers for the Arts.

6. Chicago also credits art critic Lucy Lippard with provoking change in her artwork. She discussed this with Norma Broude and Mary D. Garrard in "Conversations with Judy Chicago and Miriam Schapiro," *The Power of Feminist Art: The American Movement of the 1970s, History and Impact*, eds. Norma Broude and Mary D. Garrard (New York: Abrams, 1994), 70.

7. The word "collaboration," as applied to Chicago's work is controversial. Some writers have termed her methods cooperative, rather than collaborative. Others have accused her of attempting to set up an atelier in which she occupied the role of "master." Some have sarcastically referred to her use of volunteerism. However, collaboration simply indicates that work is done in association with others, that tasks are performed together. Such criticisms of Chicago's methods can stem from the writer's misunderstanding of the fluidity of the term, a nonacceptance of the possible permutations of a collaborative process, the insertion of the writer's version of an "ideal" form of collaboration into the discussion of the processes associated with Judy Chicago's art-making, or a projection of the writer's own hierarchical assumptions. For a summary discussion of some of these criticisms see: Amelia Jones, "The 'Sexual Politics' of *The Dinner Party*: A Critical Context," *Sexual Politics: Judy Chicago's Dinner Party in Feminist Art History*, ed. Amelia Jones (Los Angeles: UCLA at the Armand Hammer Museum of Art, 1996), 103–108.

8. Broude and Garrard, 70.

9. Chicago, *The Dinner Party: Symbol*, 240.

10. This breaking of an accepted tradition may be one source of criticism for Chicago's working relationships. In essence, Chicago's practice reveals the truth about many artists working in the past and today. For example, a painting from the work-

shop of a past master is often simply associated with the master. Many contemporaries have used collaborators and technical staff without crediting them. In part, Chicago may suffer criticism on this account simply because her practice of crediting her collaborators puts her in the position of an art world critic.

11. Gordon J. Hazlitt, "'An Incredibly Beautiful Quandary,'" *ARTnews*, May 1976, 38.

12. Chicago, *Birth Project*, 7.

13. Some additional media was utilized and a few other collaborators joined Chicago and Woodman in the *Holocaust Project*. Several examples follow: the weaver, Audrey Cowan, completed the modified Aubusson tapestry, *The Fall*, from Chicago's full-scale painted cartoon; the stained-glass logo combined the efforts of Michael Caudle, Bob Gomez, Flo Perkins, Donald Woodman, and Judy Chicago.

14. Carol Duncan, "Virility and Domination in Early Twentieth-Century Vanguard Painting," *Feminism and Art History: Questioning the Litany*, eds. Norma Broude and Mary D. Garrard (New York: Harper and Row, 1982), 306. Vlaminck's remarks can be found in: Herschel B. Chipp, *Theories of Modern Art: A Source Book by Artists and Critics* (Berkeley, Los Angeles, London: University of California Press, 1968), 144.

15. Chicago, *Holocaust Project*, 10.

16. Laura Meyer, "From Finish Fetish to Feminism: Judy Chicago's *Dinner Party* in California Art History," *Sexual Politics: Judy Chicago's Dinner Party in Feminist Art History*, ed. Amelia Jones (Los Angeles: UCLA at the Armand Hammer Museum of Art, 1996), 71.

17. Judy Chicago, Introductory Panels, the *Birth Project* exhibitions.

18. Broude and Garrard, 70–71.

19. Previous to this Chicago had taken a separatist approach with the founding of the Feminist Art Program at Fresno State College in 1970 and she, Miriam Schapiro, and Faith Wilding spoke about female imagery in a 1971 issue of *Everywoman*. It is significant that in Judith Dancoff's interview with Chicago for the issue, Chicago surmised a "cultural" source for "female imagery." Judith Dancoff, "Interview with Judy Chicago," *Everywoman*, 7 May 1971, 4–5.

20. Miriam Schapiro and Judy Chicago, "Female Imagery," *Womanspace Journal*, Summer 1973, 11–14.

21. Norma Broude and Mary D. Garrard, "Introduction: The Expanding Discourse," *The Expanding Discourse: Feminism and Art History*, eds. Norma Broude and Mary D. Garrard (New York: HarperCollins, 1992), 6. Broude and Garrard write that they reject "modernism vs. post-modernism, essentialism vs. constructivism, theory vs. practice."

22. Irving Sandler, *Art of the Postmodern Era: From the Late 1960s to the Early 1990s* (New York: Icon Editions, 1996), 546.

23. For example, Marilyn Stokstad, *Art History* (New York: Abrams, 1995), 1149–1167.

24. Kenneth Clark, *The Nude: A Study in Ideal Form* (New York: MJF Books, 1956), 4. Clark analyzed nudes by male artists only.

25. John Berger, *Ways of Seeing* (London: British Broadcasting Corporation and Penguin, 1972), 56.

26. Mary D. Garrard, "Artemisia and Susanna," *Feminism and Art History: Questioning the Litany*, eds. Norma Broude and Mary D. Garrard (New York: Harper and Row, 1982), 146–171.

27. Duncan, 292–313.

28. Whitney Chadwick, *Women, Art, and Society* (London: Thames and Hudson, 1990), 282.

29. Joanna Frueh, "The Body Through Women's Eyes," *The Power of Feminist Art: The American Movement of the 1970s, History and Impact*, eds. Norma Broude and Mary D. Garrard (New York: Abrams, 1994), 190–207.

30. Josephine Withers, "Judy Chicago's 'Birth Project': A Feminist Muddle?" *New Art Examiner*, January 1986, 29.

31. Approximately 8000 to 2000 B.C. in what is now part of southeastern Europe.

32. There are other women who have made a point of painting the male nude from a decidedly female perspective. For example, Sylvia Sleigh painted her nude male-inhabited *The Turkish Bath* (1973) as a serious spoof of Ingres's well-known painting. Alice Neel painted Joe Gould, a New York poet and sexual exhibitionist, freakishly with three sets of genitals. An interest in a portrayal of men by women is evidenced by such exhibitions as the 1980 *Women's Images of Men* shown at the Institute of Contemporary Art in London.

33. Paula Harper, *Powerplay* (New York: ACA Galleries, 1986), 3.

34. Harper, 10.

35. Harper, 19.

36. Harper, 19.

37. Postmodernism views Western societal systems of power within a hierarchic positioning of binary opposites, like male and female. Feminist theologians have defined, more holistically, a Western societal hierarchical model as emanating from the Judeo-Christian identification of God as male. Thus higher power resides in men as God's representatives, and power extends hierarchically downward over women who traditionally must relate to God through men. The structure provides a further model for a continuation of power over "others," such as over other peoples identified by characteristics like age or race, or over animals and nature, and so on.

38. Clifford Geertz, "Religion as a Cultural System," *Reader in Comparative Religion: An Anthropological Approach*, eds. William A. Lessa and Evon Z. Vogt, 2nd ed. (New York: Harper and Row, 1965), 206, 208. Feminist theologian, Carol Christ, has acknowledged Geertz's contribution in a number of publications. For example, in the *Rebirth of the Goddess: Finding Meaning in Feminist Spirituality* she states, "The deep values and the way of life of a culture, its mythos and ethos, are interdependent, as anthropologist Clifford Geertz has taught us to see." (Reading, MA: Addison-Wesley Publishing, 1997), 160.

39. John Richardson, "Strictly from Hunger," *The New York Review of Books*, 30 April 1981, 18.

40. Robert Hughes writes in *American Visions: The Epic History of Art in America* (New York: Alfred A. Knopf, 1997), 618: " . . . [T]ribalists and fundamentalists . . . credit art with power it does not have (but which the political 'vanguard' nostalgically wishes it had): that of literally changing behavior and reality."

41. Through the Flower Corporation, "Celebrating the *Birth Project* Staff," The *Birth Project Newsletter*, Fall 1983, 9.

COMPLETE BIBLIOGRAPHY

BY JUDY CHICAGO

Chicago, Judy. *Beyond the Flower: The Autobiography of a Feminist Artist*. New York: Viking/Penguin, 1996.

Chicago, Judy. *Birth Project*. New York: Doubleday/Anchor, 1985.

Chicago, Judy. *The Dinner Party*. New York: Viking/Penguin, 1996.

Chicago, Judy. *The Dinner Party: A Symbol of Our Heritage*. New York: Doubleday/Anchor, 1979.

Chicago, Judy. *Embroidering Our Heritage: The Dinner Party Needlework*, New York: Doubleday/Anchor, 1980.

Chicago, Judy. *Holocaust Project: From Darkness into Light*. New York: Viking/Penguin, 1993.

Chicago, Judy. *Judy Chicago: The Dinner Party*, Germany: Athenaum, 1987.

Chicago, Judy. "Merger Poem." Appears in Graff, Ann O'Hara, ed. *In the Embrace of God: Feminist Approaches to Theological Anthropology*. New York: Orbis Books, 1995.

Chicago, Judy. "Merger Poem." Appears in Bilson, Barbara, Rabbi Sue Levi Elwell, Marlene Gilbert, William Gluckman, James Greenwood, Rabbi Sanford Ragins, Betty Rosenfeld, Nancy Sogg, and Cantor William Sharlin. Leo Baeck Temple Shabbat Service. Los Angeles: Leo Baeck Temple, 1995.

Chicago, Judy. "Merger Poem." Appears in Berman, Rabbi Donna. *Passover Haggadah*. New York: Port Jewish Center, 1995.

Chicago, Judy. *Through the Flower: My Struggle as a Woman Artist*, New York: Doubleday, 1975; New York: Anchor, 1977; revised edition, 1982; Japan: Parco, 1979; England: Women's Press, 1982; Germany: Verlag (neue frau), *Dirch die Blume*, 1984; New York: Penguin, 1993; Taiwan: Yuan-Liou Publishing Company, Ltd., 1997.

Chicago, Judy and Edward Lucie-Smith. *Women and Art: Contested Territory*. New York: Watson-Guptill, 1999.

BOOKS

Adams, Clinton. *Printmaking in New Mexico*. Albuquerque: University of New Mexico Press, 1991.

Adams, Laurie Schneider. *The Methodologies of Art*. New York: HarperCollins, 1996.

Adams, Laurie Schneider. *A History of Western Art*. Second edition. London: Brown & Benchmark, 1997.

Aigen, Ronald, ed. *Renew Our Days*. Montreal: The Reconstructionist Synagogue of Montreal, 1996.

American Art Book, The. London: Phaidon Press Limited, 1999.

Antler, Joyce. *The Journey Home: Jewish Women and the American Century*. New York: Free Press, 1997.

Barasch, Moshe, and Lucy Freeman Sandler, eds. *Art, the Ape of Nature: Essays in Honor of H. W. Janson*. "Judy Chicago's *The Dinner Party*: A Personal Vision of Women's History," by Josephine Withers. New York: Harry N. Abrams, 1981.

Battcock, Gregory, ed. *Minimal Art: A Critical Anthology*. New York: E. P. Dutton & Co., 1968.

Bernikow, Louise. *American Women's Almanac*. New York: Berkley Books, 1997.

Bersson, Robert. *World of Art*. San Francisco: Mayfield Publishing, 1991.

Betterton, Rosemary. *Looking On: Images of Femininity in the Visual Arts and Media*. New York: Pandora Press, 1987.

Blake, Nayland, Lawrence Rinder, and Amy Scholder, eds. *In a Different Light*. San Francisco: City Lights Books, 1995.

Bohm-Duchen, Monica, and Janet Cook. *Understanding Modern Art*. London: Usborne Publishing, 1991.

Bond, Edward. *Coffee* (cover illustration). England: Methuen Drama, 1995.

Borzello, Frances. *A World of Our Own: Women Artists Since the Renaissance*. New York: Watson-Guptill, 2000.

Bratenberg, Gerd. *Le figlie di Egalia*. Borgo Pinti: Estro Editrice, 1977, 1991.

Brenner, Rachel Feldhay. *Writing as Resistance: Four Women Confronting the Holocaust* (cover illustration). University Park, Pennsylvania: Pennsylvania State University Press, 1997.

Brommer, Gerald F. *Discovering Art History*. Third edition. Worcester, MA: Davis Publications, 1997.

Brommer, Gerald F., and George Horn. *Art in Your Visual Environment*. Worcester, MA: Davis Publications, 1985.

Broude, Norma, and Mary D. Garrard, eds. *The Expanding Discourse: Feminism and Art History*. New York: HarperCollins, 1992.

Broude, Norma, and Mary D. Garrard, eds. *The Power of Feminist Art: The American Movement of the 1970s, History and Impact*. New York: Harry N. Abrams, 1994.

Brown, Betty Ann, ed. *Expanding Circles: Women, Art, and Community*. New York: Midmarch Arts Press, 1996.

Buser, Thomas. *Experiencing Art Around Us*. St. Paul, MN: West Publishing, 1995.

Button, John. *The Cassell Handbook of Radicalism*. England: Cassell, 1995.

Chadwick, Whitney. *Women, Art and Society*. London: Thames and Hudson, 1990.

Chesler, Phyllis, Esther Rothblum, and Ellen Cole, eds. *Feminist Foremothers in Women's Studies, Psychology, and Mental Health*. New York: Hawthorne Press, 1995.

Cooks, Robert, and Karla Baur. *Our Sexuality*. Fourth edition. Redwood City, CA: Benjamin/Cummings Publishing, 1990.

Covey, Alan, ed. *A Century of Women*. Atlanta: TBS Books, 1994.

Craven, Wayne. *American Art: History and Culture*. Madison, WI: Brown & Benchmark, 1994.

Creighton-Kelly, Chris, ed. *Fear of Others: Art Against Racism*. Vancouver: Arts in Action Society, 1989.

Danby, Susan, ed. *Language as Object: Emily Dickinson and Contemporary Art*. Amherst, MA: Mead Art Museum, Amherst College, University of Massachusetts Press, 1997.

Davis, Bruce. *Made in L.A. The Prints of Cirrus Editions*. Los Angeles: Los Angeles County Museum of Art, 1995.

Dawtrey, Liz, Toby Jackson, Mary Masterson, Pam Meecham, and Paul Wood, eds. *Investigating Modern Art*. Milton Keynes, England: Open University Press, 1996.

De La Croix, Horst, Richard G. Tansey, and Diane Kirkpatrick. *Gardner's Art Through The Ages*. Ninth edition. New York: Harcourt Brace Jovanovich, 1991.

Donahue, M. Patricia. *Nursing: An Illustrated History of the Finest Art*. St. Louis: Mosby, 1988. Roma: Antonio Delfino Editore, 1991.

Donahue, M. Patricia. *Nursing, The Finest Art: An Illustrated History*. Second edition. St. Louis, MO: Mosby, 1996.

Edney, Andrew. *Cat: Wild Cats and Pampered Pets*. New York: Watson-Guptill, 1999.

Eidelberg, Martin. *Designed for Delight: Alternative Aspects of 20th Century Decorative Arts*. Paris/New York: Montreal Museum of Decorative Arts in association with Flammarion, 1997.

Epstein, Vivian Sheldon. *History of Women Artists for Children*. Denver: VSE Publisher, 1987.

Ergas, Aimée G., ed. *Artists: From Michelangelo to Maya Lin*. Farmington Hills, MI: Gale Research, 1995.

Fichner-Rathus, Lois. *Understanding Art*. Fifth edition. Englewood Cliffs, NJ: Prentice-Hall, 1998.

Fichner-Rathus, Lois. *Understanding Art*. Second edition. Englewood Cliffs, NJ: Prentice-Hall, 1988.

Fiero, Gloria K. *The Humanistic Tradition*. Second edition. Madison, WI: Brown & Benchmark, 1995.

Finlayon, Judith. *The New Woman's Diary*. New York: Crown Publishers, 1993.

Fitch, Noel Riley. *Anais: The Erotic Life of Anais Nin*. Boston: Little, Brown & Co., 1993.

Foner, Moe, ed. *Images of Labor*. New York: Pilgrim Press, 1981.

Ford-Grasbowsky, Mary, ed. *Prayers for All People*. New York: Doubleday Publishing Group, 1995.

Foss, Karen, and Sonja Foss. *Women Speak: The Eloquence of Women's Lives*. Prospect Heights, IL: Waveland Press, 1991.

Frankel, David, ed. *Sniper's Nest: Art That Has Lived with Lucy R. Lippard*. New York: Bard College, 1996.

Freeman, Julian. *Art: A Crash Course*. New York: Watson-Guptill Publications, 1998.

Frost-Knappman, Elizabeth. *The ABC-CLIO Companion to Women's Progress in America*. Santa Barbara: ABC-CLIO, 1994.

Frueh, Joanna, Laurie Fierstein and Judith Stein. *Picturing the Amazon*. New Museum Books. New York: Rizzoli International Publications, Inc., 2000.

Gadon, Elinor. *Once and Future Goddess*. San Francisco: Harper & Row, 1989.

Gaze, Delia. *Dictionary of Women Artists*, vol 2. Chicago: Fitzroy Dearborn, 1997.

George, Demetra. *Mysteries of the Dark Moon: The Healing Power of the Dark Goddess*. New York: HarperCollins, 1992.

Gilbert, Rita. *Living with Art*. Third edition. New York: McGraw-Hill, 1991.

Gilbert, Rita, and William McCarter. *Living with Art*. New York: Alfred A. Knopf, 1988.

Goldberg, Roselee. *Performance: Live Art Since 1960*. New York: Harry N. Abrams, Inc., 1998.

Goodman, Lizbeth, ed. *Literature and Gender*. London: Open University Press, 1996.

Graham, Laniet. *Goddesses*. New York: Abbeville Press Publishers, 1997.

Henry, Madeleine M. *Prisoner of History*. New York: Oxford University Press, 1995.

Herberholz, Donald, and Barbara Herberholz. *Artworks for Elementary Teachers*. Madison, WI: Brown & Benchmark, 1994.

Hessel, Carolyn Starman, ed. *Blessed Is the Daughter*. New York: Shengold Books, 1999.

Hobbs, Jack A. *Art in Context*. Third edition. New York: Harcourt Brace Jovanovich, 1985.

Honour, Hugh, and John Fleming. *A World History of Art*, Fifth edition. London: Laurence King Publishing, 1999.

Hopkins, David, *After Modern Art 1945–2000*. Oxford, England: Oxford University Press, 2000.

Hopkins, Henry. *Fifty West Coast Artists*. San Francisco: Chronicle Books, 1981.

Horisch, Jochen. *Brot und Wein*. Frankfurt: Edition Suhrkamp, 1992.

Horowitz, Frederick A. *More Than You See*. New York: Harcourt Brace Jovanovich, 1985.

Hubbard, Guy. *Art in Action*. San Diego: Coronado Publishers, 1987.

Hughes, James. *The Larousse Desk Reference*. New York: Larousse Kingfisher Chambers, 1995.

Hunter College Women's Studies Collective. *Women's Realities, Women's Choices*. Second edition. New York: Oxford University Press, 1995.

Information Design Series: A Sea of Information vol. 6. Tokyo: Kadokawa Shoten Publishing Co., Ltd., 2000.

International Ceramics Public Art Exhibition. Taipei County: Taipei County Cultural Center, 1998.

Israel, Glenis. *Artwise: visual arts 7–10*. Milton, Queensland: Jacaranda, 1997.

Jones, Amelia, ed. *Sexual Politics: Judy Chicago's Dinner Party in Feminist Art History*. Los Angeles: UC Press, 1996.

Jones, Suzanne, ed. *Writing the Woman Artist: Essays on Poetics, Politics and Portraiture*. Pennsylvania: University of Pennsylvania Press, 1991.

Kimball, Gayle. *Women's Culture: The Women's Renaissance of the Seventies*. Metuchen, NJ/London: The Scarecrow Press, 1981.

Kissick, John. *ART: Context and Criticism*. Madison, WI: Brown & Benchmark, 1993.

Klien, Wymer, and Edwards. *Great Ideas: Conversations Between Past and Present*. Fort Worth, TX: Holt, Rinehart and Winston, 1991.

Kramarae, Cheris, ed. *Technology and Women's Voices: Keeping in Touch*. New York: Routledge & Kegan Paul, 1988.

Kubitza, Anette. *Die Kunst, das Loch, die Frau: Feministische Kontroversen um Judy Chicago's Dinner Party*. Pfaffenweiler, Germany: Centaurus-Verlagsgesellschaft, 1994.

Kubitza, Anette. *Judy Chicago's The Dinner Party Im Kontext Feministischer Diskurse*. Wissenschaftliche Hausarbeit zur Erlangung des akademischen Grades eines Magister Artium der Universitat Hamburg. Hamburg, Germany, 1991.

Lande, Marilyn. *Jewish Women: Their History and Relationships to the Visual Arts*. Denver: Central Agency for Jewish Education, 1990.

Langdon, Ann. *Women Visual Artists You Might Like to Know*. New Haven, CT: William J. Mack, 1990.

Lacy, Suzanne, ed. *Mapping the Terrain: Genre Public Art*. Seattle, WA: Bay Press, 1995.

Lewis, Richard, and Susan I. Lewis. *The Power of Art*. Fort Worth, TX: Harcourt Brace Jovanovich, 1995.

Lippard, Lucy. "Drawing on Strength" from *Trials and Tributes*. Tallahassee, FL: Florida State University, 1999.

Lippard, Lucy. *From the Center: Feminist Essays on Women's Art*. New York: Dutton, 1976.

Lippard, Lucy. *The Pink Glass Swan: Selected Essays on Art*. New York: New Press, 1995.

Lippard, Lucy. *Overlay: Contemporary Art and the Art of Prehistory*. New York: New Press, 1983.

Lordahl, Jo Ann. *The End of Motherhood: New Identities, New Lives*. Deerfield Beach, FL: Health Communications, 1990.

Lucie-Smith, Edward. *Adam: The Male Figure in Art*. London: Weidenfeld & Nicolson, 1998.

Lucie-Smith, Edward. *Art and Civilization*. Englewood Cliffs, NJ: Prentice-Hall, 1992.

Lucie-Smith, Edward. *Judy Chicago: An American Vision*. New York: Watson-Guptill Publications, 2000.

Lucie-Smith, Edward. *Zoo*. London: Aurum Press, 1998.

Martin, Katherine. *Women of Courage: Inspiring Stories from the Women Who Lived Them*. Novoto, CA: New World Library, 1999.

Matthews, Roy T., and F. DeWitt Platt. *The Western Humanities*. Second edition. Mountain View, CA: Mayfield Publishing, 1995.

Milinaire, Catherine. *Birth*. New York: Harmony Books, 1987.

Mirus, Helma, and Erika Wisselinck, eds. *Mit Mut und Phantasie*. Strasslach, Germany: Sophia Verlag, 1987.

Montreynaud, Florence. *Le XXe Siecle Des Femmes*. Paris: Editions Nathan, 1989.

Moure, Nancy Dustin Wall. *California Art: 450 Years of Painting and Other Media*. Los Angeles: Dustin, 1998.

Munro, Eleanor. *Originals: American Women Artists*. New York: Simon & Schuster, 1979.

Muten, Burleigh, ed. *Return of the Goddess*. New York: Stewart, Tabori & Chang, 1999.

Muten, Burleigh, ed. *Return of the Great Goddess*. Boston: Shambhala Publications, 1994.

Nittve, Lars, and Helle Grenzien, eds. *Sunshine Noir: Art in L.A. 1960–1997*. Humbleback, Denmark: Museum of Modern Art, 1998.

Odysseia Textbook. Helsinki: Edita, 2000.

Panzacchi, Cornelia. *A World of Our Own*. London: Thames and Hudson, 2000.

Peterson, Susan. *The Craft and Art of Clay*. Englewood Cliffs, NJ: Prentice-Hall, 1992.

Phillips, Lisa. *The American Century: Art and Culture 1950–2000*. New York: W. W. Norton & Company, 2000.

Phipps, Richard. *Invitation to the Gallery*. Dubuque, IA: William C. Brown Publishers, 1987.

Preble, Duane, and Sarah and Patrick Frank. *Artforms*. New York: Longman, 1999.

Raven, Arlene. *At Home*. Long Beach, CA: Long Beach Museum, 1983.

Raven, Arlene. *Crossing Over: Feminism and Art of Social Concern*. Ann Arbor, MI: UMI Research Press, 1988.

Remer, Amy. *Pioneering Spirits*. Worcester, MA: Davis Publications, 1997.

Reid, Robert Leonard. *America, New Mexico*. Tucson, AZ: University of Arizona Press, 1998.

Richardson, John. *Sacred Monsters, Sacred Masters*. New York: Random House, 2001.

Robinson, Hilary, ed. *Visibly Female: Feminism and Art Today*. New York: Universe Books, 1988.

Roth, Moira, ed. *Conversations: Interviews with 28 Bay Area Women Artists*. Oakland, CA: Mills College, 1988.

Roundtree, Cathleen. *Coming into Our Fullness: On Turning Forty*. Freedom, CA: Crossing Press, 1991.

Rubinstein, Charlotte. *American Women Sculptors: A History of Women Working in Three Dimensions*. Boston: G.K. Hall & Co., 1990.

Rugoff, Ralph. *Scene of the Crime*. Los Angeles: UCLA at the Armand Hammer Museum of Art and Cultural Center, 1997.

Russell, Carol. *The Tapestry Handbook*. Asheville, NC: Lark Books, 1990.

Russell, Stella Pandell. *Art in the World*. Second edition. New York: Holt, Reinhart and Winston, 1984.

Russell, Stella Pandell. *Art in the World*. Fourth edition. New York: Harcourt Brace Jovanovich, 1993.

Sandler, Irving. *Art of the Postmodern Era*. New York: HarperCollins, 1996.

Sayre, Henry M. *The Object of Performance*. Chicago: University of Chicago Press, 1989.

Schneider, Dorothy, and Carl J. Schneider. *The ABC-CLIO Companion to Women in the Workplace*. Santa Barbara, CA: ABC-CLIO, 1993.

Seigel, Judy, ed. *Mutiny and the Mainstream: Talk That Changed Art, 1975–1990*. New York: Midmarch Arts Press, 1991.

Slatkin, Wendy. *Women Artists in History*. Upper Saddle River, NJ: Prentice-Hall, 1989.

Soussloff, Catherine M., ed. *Jewish Identity in Modern Art History*. Berkeley: University of California Press, 1999.

Stokstad, Marilyn. *Art History*. New York: Harry N. Abrams, 1995.

Stoops, Susan L., ed. *More Than Minimal: Feminism and Abstraction in the 70's*. Waltham, MA: Rose Art Museum, Brandeis University, 1996.

Strong, Brian, and Christine DeVault. *Human Sexuality*. Mountain View, CA: Mayfield Publishing, 1994.

Tansey, Richard G., and Fred S. Kleiner. *Gardner's Art Through the Ages*. Tenth edition. Fort Worth, TX: Harcourt Brace Jovanovich, 1996.

Taylor, Brandon. *Avant-Garde and After: Rethinking Art Now*. New York: Harry N. Abrams, 1995.

Theisen, Michael. *Sexuality: Challenges and Choices*. Winona, MN: Christian Brothers Publications, 1995.

Thornton, Shapiro Jill. *A Women's Seder*. Atlantic, GA: Jill Schapiro Thornton, 1996.

Todey, Susan. *The Art of Motherhood*. New York: Abbeville Press, 1990.

Twentieth Century Art Book, The. London: Phaidon Press Limited, 1996.

Vanceburg, Martha. *A New Life: Daily Readings for a Happy Healthy Pregnancy*. New York: Bantam Books, 1990.

Von Blum, Paul. *Other Visions, Other Voices*. Lanham, MD: University Press of America, 1994.

Warr, Tracy and Amelia Jones. *The Artist's Body*. London: Phaidon, 2000.

Weigle, Martha. *Creation and Procreation-Feminist Reflections on Cosmogony and Parturition*. Philadelphia: University of Pennsylvania, 1989.

Wetzel, Jodi, et al. *Women's Studies; Thinking Women*. Dubuque, IA: Kendall/Hunt Publishing, 1993.

Witt, Mary Ann Frese, et al. *The Humanities: Cultural Roots and Continuities*. Fifth edition. vol. II. Boston: Houghton Mifflin, 1997.

Witt, Mary Ann Frese, et al. *The Humanities*. Third edition. vol. II. Lexington, MA: D.C. Heath and Company, 1989.

Witzling, Mara, ed. *Voicing Our Visions: Writings by Women Artists*. New York: Universe, 1991.

Wolff, Janet. *Postmodernism and Society*. London: Macmillan, 1990.

Wylder, Viki D. Thompson. *Trials and Tributes* (exhibition catalog). Tallahassee, FL: Florida State University, 1999.

Ziesche, Angela. *Das Schwere und das Leichte*. Koln, Germany: DuMont, 1995.

Zophy, Angela Howard, ed. *Handbook of American Women's History*. New York: Garland Publishing, 1990.

ARTICLES

2001

Wylder, Viki D. Thompson Ph.D. "New Orleans Museum of Art-Judy Chicago: Trials and Tributes." *Arts Quarterly* 23, no. 1 (January/February/March 2001).

2000

Abrams, Carol K. "Landmark Exhibits at 2 HUC Campuses," *Cleveland Jewish News*, 15 December 2000.

Andre, Mila. "Hurry, This Crafts Menagerie Won't Last." *Daily News* (New York), 18 August 2000.

Barber, Christina. "Chicago's (Dinner) Party Isn't Over." *Daily Hampshire Gazette* (Northampton, MA), 18 May 2000, sec. D:1.

Brannock, Amy. "Judy Chicago: Artist in Residence This Fall at UNC and Duke." *Arts Carolina* (Fall 2000).

Brock, Lisa A. "Post-Feminism? 'Ridiculous'." *The Minnesota Women's Press*, vol. 16, no. 15 (2000).

Budick, Ariella. "Chicago Explores Values with 'A Stitch in Time'." *Newsday*, 9 June 2000.

"Chicago's Artwork Packs a Principled Punch." *Tampa Tribune*, 9 January 2000, Baylife sec. 70.

Cicek, Filiz. "Cumhuriyet Dergi Pazareki" (Turkish Newspaper), 28 May 2000.

Duffy, L.A. "Lunch with Judy Chicago at ERA's 26th Anniversary." *Bay Area Business Woman*, vol. 7, no. 9 (June 2000): 3.

Grapheion, no. 13 (2000): 42, 46.

Greenberg, Blue. "Chicago's Art Honors Women in History." *The Herald-Sun* (Durham, NC), 20 October 2000, sec. D:4.

Halperen, Max. "Artist's Work Is Never Done." *The News and Observer*, 1 October 2000, sec. G Arts and Entertainment.

Harper, Paula. "The Chicago Resolutions." *Art in America*, (June 2000): 112–115.

"Holocaust Exhibit a Semester Long Project." *Lehigh Week*, 26 January 2000.

Jameson, Marnell. "Teaching Humanities as a Life Skill." *Los Angeles Times*, 6 June 2000, sec. E, Southern California Living.

Johnson, Ken. "Offering Up Good Cheer and the Humanist Values, All Rendered in Clichés." *New York Times*, 4 August 2000, sec. E:6.

"Judy Chicago Uses Age Old Crafts in Contemporary Art Installation." *Antiques and The Arts Weekly*, 12 May 2000, 93.

"Judy Chicago's *Birth Project* on Display Daily at Albuquerque Museum Through October 29." *Valencia County News Bulletin*, 30 August 2000, Arts and Leisure sec. C.

"Judy Chicago in Residence at Lehigh University." *Art Matters*, (March 2000): 7.

Martin, Nedene. "Meet Our Woman of the Weekend: The 12th Century Star Eleanor de Aquitaine." *Vermont Humanities* (Fall 2000): 16.

McNamara, Eileen. "Reach for the Stars, Let Balance Guide Steps to Life Goals." *Times Union* (Albany, NY), 22 May 2000, sec. A:7.

McNamara, Eileen. "Women Grads Get Wrong Idea." *The Boston Globe*, 17 May 2000.

Potts, Leanne. "Chicago Hope." *Albuquerque Tribune*, 11 August 2000, sec. C:3.

Pulkka, Wesley. "Exhibition of Jewish Artwork Expands Past Original Ideas." *Albuquerque Journal*, 4 June 2000.

"Resolutions: A Stitch in Time." *Museum News*, M Calendar, 2000.

"Rich in Art." *Floridian*, 7 January 2000, sec. D:1.

Russell, Gloria. "The Many Sides of Judy Chicago." *Sunday Republican* (Springfield, MA), 21 May 2000, sec. G:2.

Sanchez-Morantz, Regina. "Artist-in-Residence Judy Chicago Presents NEH-Trustee Lecture on Tolerance." *Philip and Muriel Berman Center for Jewish Studies Newsletter*, vol. 13 (Fall 2000).

Smith Alumnae Quarterly. "Commencement 2000: Artist Judy Chicago Gives Grads a Reality Check." *Banks of Paradise* (Fall 2000).

Steinberg, David. "Local Icon." *Albuquerque Journal*, 4 June 2000.

"Through Women's Eyes." *Tampa Tribune*, 9 January 2000, sec. 1 Baylife.

"To Deconstruct Her Is to Know Her." *Floridian*, 7 January 2000, sec. D:3.

Weinraub, Bernard. "Beyond Tans and Tinsel." *New York Times*, 23 October 2000, sec. B:1.

Wilensky, Melody. "Radical Smith Speaker Engages Tradition, Commencement Speaker Turns Toward Ritual in Feminist Art Movement." *The Jewish Advocate*, vol. 190, no. 20, 19–25 May 2000, sec. 1A–21A.

Wilgoren, Jodi. "Words of Advice for Graduates on the Threshold of the Millennium." *New York Times*, 29 May 2000, sec. A (National) 11.

1999

Alt, Jeanette. "Judy Chicago," *Santa Fean*, Gallery Previews (June 1999): 78.

Bakke, Kristin M. "Chicago Comes to Bloomington." *Indiana Daily Student*, 9 September 1999.

Bakke, Kristin M. "Feminist Artist to Return to IU-B Campus." *The IUPUI Sagamore*, 13 September 1999, 1, 10.

Bakke, Kristin M. "Influential Artist to Teach at IU." *Indiana Daily Student*, vol. 132, issue 76 (September 1999).

Berry, S.L. "Art with Attitude." *The Indianapolis Star*, 26 September 1999, 1–2.

Brand, Peg. "Judy Chicago's Art and Presence Resulting in Interest and Education," *The Herald-Times*, 15 October 1999.

Bright, Kimberly. "A Life in Art." *Bloomington Independent*, 16 September 1999: 13.

Cavalli, Ellen. "Judy Chicago Reaches Out in New Direction," *Pasatiempo*, 4–10 June 1999, 14.

Chen, Elsa H.C. "Women in Art." *Art China*, no. 7, 1 April 1999.

"Conversation with . . . Judy Chicago, co-author of *Women and Art, Contested Territory*," *Today's Librarian* (December 1999): 16.

Falkenstein, Michelle. "What's So Good About Being Bad." *ARTnews*, (November 1999): 159–163.

Finkelstein, Lydia B. "Taking a Look Back at the Career of Judy Chicago." *Sunday Herald-Times*, 19 September 1999, sec. D:7.

Frank, Johanna. "Judy Chicago: Bridging Feminism and the Art World." *The Ryder* (September 1999): 26–29.

Henderson, Michelle. "Judy Chicago to Visit IU Art Museum." *Sunday Herald-Times*, 12 September 1999, sec. D:1, 5.

"Hide in Plain Sight," *ARTnews* (April 1999): 27.

Home Pages: Indiana University, vol. 4, issue 2, 17 September 1999, 1.

"International Artists to Sign Books at Herron," *The IUPUI Sagamore*, 13 September 1999, 6.

Koba, Kirsten. "Chicagoland." *Ms.* (October–November 1999): 87.

Kunstbeeld, (November 1999): 42–45.

Mannheimer, Steve. "Judy Chicago's Work Is Art to Dissect and Digest." *The Indianapolis Star*, 3 October 1999, 13.

Morrison, Richard. "Week in the Arts." *The London Times*, 26 October 1999.

Neal, Andrea. "Feminist Draws Fire at IU," *The Indianapolis Star*, 14 October 1999.

Rhea, Tom. "Personal Monuments: Judy Chicago Retrospective Opens at Indiana University Art Museum" *Bloomington Independent*, 2 September 1999: 15–16.

Saltzstein, Katherine. "Judy Chicago Recreates Hill in Watercolor," *Valencia County News-Bulletin*. vol. 89, no. 46, 9–10 June 1999.

"Ten Works of Art That Have Rocked the Ages." *Newsweek*, 11 October 1999: 70.

"What Are You Doing New Year's Eve?" *St. Petersburg Times*, 31 December 1999, 29W.

Whitehead, John W. "Women and Art: An Interview with Judy Chicago." *Gadfly* (November/December 1999): 44–49.

Williams, Kevin. M. "Woman." *Chicago Sun-Times*, 22 October 1999.

Yu, San-San. "To Break Silence of a Sixty-Million-Year Taboo." *Art China*, no. 7, 1 April 1999.

1998

Battin, Sandy. "A Stitch in Time." *Valencia County News-Bulletin*, 11–12 July 1998, sec. B:1.

Bellafonte, Ginia. "Feminism: It's All About Me." *Time*, 29 June 1998, 54–62.

Chicago, Judy. "A Journey of Discovery." *NCJW Journal* 21, no. 1 (Spring 1998): 16–17.

Miller, Stephen. "A Note on the Banality of Evil." *The Wilson Quarterly* (Autumn 1998): 54–59.

Moore, Derrickson. "Judy Chicago's Latest Project Looks to the Millennium." *Sun Life*, 26 July 1998, sec. C:1.

Olmstead, Donna. "Artistic Awakenings." *Journal South*, 16 July 1998: 1–2.

Rosoff, Patricia. "Cheeky Chick, I Must Say." *The Hartford Advocate*, 18 June 1998.

"Would You Wear Your Dog?" *Peta's Animal Times* (Fall 1998).

1997

Brown, Patricia. "40 Fenders and Dada in the Rearview Mirror." *New York Times*, 20 April 1997, 1, 20.

Chien, Ying-Ying. "Sexual Politics: Judy Chicago's *Dinner Party* & Feminist Art History." *Unitas* (Taipei, Taiwan) 148 (February 1997): 56–61.

Gadfly 1, no. 7 (September 1997): cover art.

Meyer, Laura. "A Monumental Meal." *Gadfly* 1, no. 7 (September 1997): 6–11, 26.

Nickell, Amy. "Judy Chicago, Creator of the Controversial Installation *The Dinner Party*." *Gadfly* 1, no. 7 (September 1997): Editorial, 4.

Nickell, Amy, and Nisha Mohammed. "Food for Thought. An Interview with Judy Chicago." *Gadfly*, 1, no. 7 (September 1997): 14–17.

Pulkka, Wesley. "Focusing Female Energy: Artist Judy Chicago's Collaborative Projects Stir Emotions, Controversy." *Albuquerque Journal*, 7 September 1997, Arts & Culture sec. F:1, 4.

Springer, Julie. "Interview with Judy Chicago." *The Bookwoman* 60, no. 3, (Spring/Summer 1997): cover art, 1–5.

Thomas, Susan Gregory. "1998 Tech Guide." *U.S. News & World Report*, 1 December 1997, 66.

Tikkun (May/June 1997): cover art.

1996

Abracarian, Robin. "The Lesson of Judy Chicago: Fame Has Its Detractions." *Los Angeles Times*, 28 April 1996, Life & Style sec. E:1–2.

"Artist, Descendant of Rabbis, Combats Evils of Holocaust." *Cleveland Plain Dealer*, 3 May 1996, Art sec. 35.

Brunskill, Joan (Associated Press). "Dinner Invitation: Artist Sets Place for Women in History," published in various papers around the United States, including *Jamestown (New York) Post-Journal*, 4 May 1996, 11.

Butruille, Susan. "Women's Voices: Past and Future . . . A Most Splendid Dinner Party." *The Women's Journal* 4, no. 8 (1996): 14.

Cantor, Judy. "Chicago Hope." *Miami New Times* 10, no. 49 (March 1996): 63, 65.

Corradi, Ruth. "Chicago in Cleveland." *Northern Ohio Live* (June 1996): 11.

Cross, Guy. "An Interview with Judy Chicago." *THE Magazine* (Santa Fe) (September 1996): 42–43.

Fernandez, Susan. "Judy Chicago: Artist and Woman." *St Petersburg Times*, 6 October 1996, Books sec. D:7.

Freese, Joan. "Open Seating: Judy Chicago Is Coming to Dinner." *The Minnesota Women's Press* 12, no. 1, 3–16 April 1996, Art sec. 28.

Heller, Fran. "*Holocaust Project*: From Darkness into Light." *Cleveland Jewish News*, 3 May 1996: 14–16.

"Journey Through the Landscape of the Holocaust, A." *New York Forward*, 6 December 1996.

Jungermann, Eva. "*Holocaust Project: From Darkness into Light*." Focus on Art (Spring 1996): 18.

Kapitanoff, Nancy. "Feminist Visions in Clay." *Ceramics: Art and Perception*, no. 25 (1996).

Kaufman, Peter, and Donna Kaufman. "Light Mixed with Darkness: Judy Chicago's *Rainbow Shabbat*." *Crosswind* (Santa Fe) (February 1996).

Knight, Christopher. "More Famine Than Feast." *Los Angeles Times*, 2 May 1996, Calendar sec. F:1.

Laughridge, Rhonda. "Judy Chicago Finds Her Heritage." *Tampa Bay Magazine* (September/October 1996): 54–55.

Lewis, Judith. "The Trouble with Judy: Reflections on *The Dinner Party* and the Artist Who Created It." *Los Angeles Weekly*, 26 April to 2 May 1996: 26–28, 30, 32, 34, 36.

McCloud, Kathleen. "Beyond *The Dinner Party*." *Santa Fe Pasatiempo*, 6–12 September 1996: 28.

Mackey, Mary. "Has the World Forgotten Judy Chicago?" *San Francisco Chronicle/Examiner*, 17 March 1996: 3.

Marger, Mary Ann. "Holocaust Exhibit Is Designed to Educate." *St Petersburg Times*, 11 October 1996, Weekend sec. W:30.

Monteagudo, Jesse. "'Flower' Still Blooms for Feminist Artist Judy Chicago." *Fort Lauderdale Sun-Sentinel*, 24 March 1996.

Muchnic, Suzanne. "Judy Chicago's *Dinner Party* Returns: Does Feminism Mean Anything Anymore?" *Los Angeles Times*, 21 April 1996, Calendar sec. 8, 9, 78, 80.

Perille, Gina. "Lewitzky Dance Company." *Dance Magazine* (October 1996).

Polak, Maralyn Lois. "A Feminist Struggles with the Boys' Club of Art." *Philadelphia Inquirer*, 5 May 1996.

Preziosi, Donald. "*Sexual Politics* an Important Show." *Los Angeles Times*, 13 May 1996, sec. F:3.

Razaire, Becky. "Holocaust Exhibit to Recognize Gay and Lesbian Victims." *Tampa Gazette*, October 1996, Suncoast sec. 7–8.

Salisbury, Wilma. "Artist's Vulnerable Side Bared." *Cleveland Plain Dealer*, 14 April 1996.

Scherzer, Amy. "Seeing Chicago." *Tampa Tribune-Times*, 6 October 1996, Baylife sec. 1.

Schillinger, Liesl. "Misunderstood as Ever." *New York Times*, 24 March 1996: 21.

Schultz, Susy. "Feast for the Eyes Back on the Road." *Chicago Sun-Times*, 5 May 1996, Mixed Media sec. B:3.

Steinberg, David. "Artist Speaks for Silenced Majority." *Albuquerque Journal*, 8 September 1996.

Sundstrom, Nancy. "Is It Art or Is It Politics?" *Traverse City Record Eagle*, 19 January 1996, Entertainment sec. D:1.

"Visual Art." *Sarasota Arts Review* (October 1996): 10.

Weinstein, Natalie. "After *Dinner Party*, Judy Chicago Feasts on Judaism." *Jewish Bulletin of Northern California*, 14 June 1996, 29–30.

Winegar, Karen. "Judy Chicago Restores Women's Place." *Minneapolis Star Tribune*, 10 April 1996, Variety sec. 1–2.

1995

Branham, Joan R. "Sacrality and Aura in the Museum: Mute Objects and Articulate Space." *The Journal of the Walters Art Gallery* 52/53 (1994/1995): 33–47.

Cotter, Holland. "Feminist Art, 1962 Until Tomorrow Morning and International." *New York Times*, 16 March 1995, sec. C:25.

Division of Labor: 'Women's Work' in Contemporary Art. Catalog for The Bronx Museum of the Arts, New York (1995).

Drohojowska-Philp, Hunter. "Prints of the City." *Los Angeles Times*, 15 October 1995, Art sec. 62.

Graham, Renee. "Why Judy Chicago Is the Artist the Art World Loves to Hate." *Boston Sunday Globe*, 24 September 1995, sec. B:27.

Hamilton, Peter. "UCLART Interviews: Judy Chicago." *UCLART Literary Art Journal*, no. 2 (Winter 1995).

Helfand, Glen. "Big Gay Art." *The Advocate*, 7 March 1995.

Jones, Amelia. "Feminist Heresies: 'Cunt Art' and the Female Body in Representation." *Heresies*, 7 February 1995.

Kahn, Sharon. "Judy Chicago's *Holocaust Project: From Darkness into Light*." *Bridges* 1, no. 5 (Summer 1995): 100–103.

Knight, Christopher. "'Women's Work' Is Never Done at MOCA." *Los Angeles Times*, 1 October 1995, Art/Art Review sec. 59, 62.

Lord, M.G. "*Women's Work* Is (Sometimes) Done." *New York Times*, 19 February 1995, sec. H:37.

"Made in L.A.: The Prints of the Cirrus Editions." *At the Museum* (October 1995): 5.

McQueen, Rachel. "Judy Chicago." *Deneuve-The Lesbian Magazine* 5, no. 6 (December 1995): Art Profile sec. 48–49.

Meyer, Laura. "Judy Chicago, Feminist Artist and Educator." *Women & Therapy: A Feminist Quarterly* 17, no. 1 and 2 (1995).

Mirrer, Judy. "Where Is Judy Chicago?" *The Flying Needle* 24, no. 1 (February 1995): 13–14.

Rodriguez, Sarah A. "From Darkness into Light." *The Harvard Crimson*, 19 October 1995.

Rosenfeld, Alvin H. "The Americanization of the Holocaust." *Commentary* (June 1995): 35–40.

Schorow, Stephanie. "Illuminating Darkness." *The Boston Herald*, 14 September 1995, Arts & Lifestyle sec. 33, 35.

Smith, Roberta. "Void, Self, Drag, Utopia (and 5 Other Gay Themes)." *New York Times*, 26 March 1995, sec. H:40.

Strickland, Carol, "Crash Course in Modern Matters." *Christian Science Monitor*, 26 October 1995.

1994

Charles, Nick. "Project Not on Critics' List: Multi-Media Holocaust Exhibit Hit." *New York Daily News*, 22 April 1994.

Cross, Guy. "Exclusive Interview with Judy Chicago." *The Magazine* (March 1994): 14–17.

Felman, Jyl Lynn. "Judy Chicago's *Holocaust Project*." *Lilith* 19, no. 2 (Summer 1994): 15–16.

Felman, Jyl Lynn. "Presentation of Evil." *Sojourner* (February 1994).

Fred, Morris. "Lessons of the *Holocaust Project* Exhibition at the Spertus Museum: First Reflections." *Council of American Jewish Museums Newsletter* (April 1994): 1, 11–12.

Gaver, Cynthia. "Judy Chicago: From Darkness into Light." *Out Smart* 1, no. 10 (15 November 1994 to 14 December 1994): 54–55.

Goldman, Saundra. "Multi-Media Artist Judy Chicago's Journey from Darkness into Light." *Austin American-Statesman*, XL ent. Magazine, 13 October 1994: cover art, 38.

"*Holocaust Project*: Judy Chicago." *Scene, London* (April–May 1994).

Hoy, Nancy Jo. "Being in the Presence of the Truth: An Interview with Judy Chicago." *The Ear*, no. 11 (Spring 1994): 26–45.

Levy, Rebecca. "Judy Chicago's *Holocaust Project*: A Time to Heal." *Austin Chronicle* 14, no. 10 (4 November 1994): 34.

Lindow, Sandra, and Michael Levy. "From Darkness into Light: Judy Chicago's *Holocaust Project*." *Kaleidoscope*, no. 29 (Summer/Fall 1994): 22–31.

Loftus, Kelley. "Long Distance: Judy Chicago." *Art Lies* (December 1994): 10–12.

Miller, Lynn C. "Life Imitates Art." *Texas Triangle* 3, no. 2, 20–26 October 1994, 7.

Monaghan, Kathleen. "Of, for, and by Georgia O'Keeffe." Catalog for Whitney Museum of American Art, New York (February 1994): 10.

Myers, Terry R. "The Mike Kelly Problem." *New Art Examiner* (Summer 1994): 24–29.

Nutkiewicz, Michael. "Watching Evolution of a Challenging Work." *Cleveland Jewish News*, 7 January 1994: 14.

O'Hara, Delia. "Chicago Spertus Museum Sees More Visitors." *Chicago Sun Times*, 3 March 1994.

"Opening Day." *Austin American-Statesman*, 17 October 1994, sec. B:1.

Parke, J. Cary. "The Heart of Darkness." *The Pink Paper* (London) (1994).

Raphael, Frederic. "On Not Keeping One's Voice Down." *TLS: Jewish Studies* (London), 6 May 1994: 7–8.

Raven, Arlene. "Judy Chicago: The Artist Art Critics Love to Hate." *On The Issues* (Summer 1994): 35–40.

Sholiton, Faye. "Judy Chicago's *Holocaust Project*." *Cleveland Jewish News*, 7 January 1994: cover art, 12–14.

Spirn, Michele. "From Darkness into Light: An Interview with Judy Chicago on the Holocaust Project." *National Council of Jewish Women Journal* 17, no. 1 (Fall 1994): cover art, 15–19.

Stamets, Bill. "The *Holocaust Project: From Darkness Into Light*." *The New Art Examiner* (March 1994).

Sweets, Ellen. "An Artist's Haunting Vision." *Dallas Morning News*, October 1994, sec. C:1, 7.

Tomchin, Susan. "Judy Chicago's Bold Look at the Holocaust." *B'nai B'rith Women's World* (Summer 1994).

Zemel, Carol. "Beyond the Reach of Art?" *Women's Review of Books* (April 1994): 6–7.

1993

"Art Spotlight." *Scholastic Art* 23, no. 5 (March 1993): 10.

"Artist Judy Chicago's *Holocaust Project*." *Lilith* 18, no. 3 (Summer 1993).

Artner, Alan. "Exploiting Pain: Judy Chicago's *Holocaust Project* Will Move Viewers." *Chicago Tribune*, 26 November 1993.

Baumgardner, Jennifer. "Judy Chicago's *Holocaust Project*." *Ms.* (November–December 1993).

Bernstein, Elizabeth. "Chicago View of Holocaust." *JUF News* (October 1993).

Cohn, Robert. "Judy Chicago Taps Neglected Roots in Her *Holocaust Project*." *St. Louis Jewish Light*, 1 December 1993.

Eauclaire, Sally. "The *Holocaust Project*." *Chicago Tribune Magazine*, 17 October 1993, sec. 10: cover, content page, 17–20.

Hess, Elizabeth. "Planet Holocaust." *Village Voice*, 2 November 1993: 43–44.

"Kustom Kulture: Von Dutch, Ed 'Big Daddy' Roth, Robert Williams and Others." Catalog for the Laguna Art Museum (1993): 88, 90.

Niederman, Sharon. "*Holocaust Project: Darkness to Light*." *Santa Fe Reporter* 18, no. 39, 17–23 March 1993: 25.

O'Hara, Delia. "Search for Roots Gives Birth to *Holocaust Project*." *Chicago Sun Times*, 20 October 1993: 43.

"A powerful chronicle of the genesis and creation of one of the most provocative exhibitions of our time: Judy Chicago's searching evocation of the Holocaust." *Jewish Book News*, 16 December 1993.

Rainbow Shabbat. *Multicultural Review* 2, no. 4: cover art.

Reed, Ollie Jr. "Confronting the Horror." *Albuquerque Tribune*, 13 April 1993, sec. D:1, 5.

Reuther, Rosemary R. "Law & Heart: God and Gaia." *The Witness* 76, no. 4 (April 1993): 24.

Steinberg, David. "Judy Chicago: Coming to Grips with Pain." *Albuquerque Journal*, 14 November 1993.

Vallongo, Sally. "Giving Life to Holocaust Art Brings Own Rebirth." *Toledo Blade*, 23 October 1993.

Woods, Linda. "The *Holocaust Project*: By Remembering the Past, We Can Change the Future." *Los Alamos* (New Mexico) *Monitor*, 18 April 1993, sec. B:1–4.

1992

"Artistic Differences." *UCLA Magazine* 3, no. 4 (Winter 1992): 24.

Epstein, Pancho. "Through the Flower." *Santa Fe New Mexican*, 24 January 1992: 20–21.

Feldman, Gayle. "FSG's 'Vindication' of the Slush Pile." *Publishers Weekly*, 12 October 1992: 20.

Mifflin, Margot. "Feminism's New Face." *ARTnews* (November 1992).

Rosen, Steven. "Local Show Previews a '93 Blockbuster." *Denver Post*, 10 May 1992, sec. D:1,4.

Sandhaas, Kari. "Birth, Choice, and the Abuse of the Sacred: A Personal Story of Resistance." *Daughters of Sarah* (Fall 1992).

"Stained Glass Window of Judy Chicago's *Holocaust Project*, The." *Stained Glass: Quarterly of the Stained Glass Association of America* 87, no. 3 (Fall 1992).

Sweets, Ellen. "Giving the Holocaust New Meaning." *Dallas Morning News*, 2 August 1992.

"20 Years of the Women's Movement." *Ms.* (1992).

1991

Carroll, Alberta. "Judy Chicago and Her Art." *Minnesota Women's Press*, 22 May 1991, 18–19.

Craven, Joan. "Canadian *Dinner Party* a Celebration." *Calgary Herald*, 4 April 1991, sec. H:5.

Danis, Naomi. "Worthy Causes." *Lilith* (Spring 1991): 32.

Eauclaire, Sally. "The Female Gaze." *Southwest Profile*, (February–April 1991): 12–14.

Eisler, Riane. "Sex, Art and Archetypes." *Women's Review of Books* 8, no. 6 (March 1991): 16.

Harrison, Helen. "No Muffling of Women's Voice." *New York Times*, 12 May 1991.

Knight, Christopher. "From Out West and the 'Cool School', It's Abstract Pop." *Los Angeles Times*, 4 April 1991, Calendar sec. 83–84.

Levy, Daniel. "Quarreling Over Quality." *Time* (Special Issue: Women: The Road Ahead), 1991: 61–62.

Lippard, Lucy. "Uninvited Guests: How Washington Lost *The Dinner Party*." *Art in America* (December 1991): 39–49.

Melendez, Michelle. "Getting Closer to the Work." *Albuquerque Journal*, 20 October 1991, sec. G:2.

Northup, JoAnn Severns. "*Finish Fetish*: LA's Cool School": *Judy Chicago*. Catalog for Fisher Gallery, University of Southern California (1991): 20–21, 27–28, 58.

Olmstead, Kim. "An Icy Reception for *The Dinner Party*." *Washington Review* (June–July 1991): 20.

Tobia, Blaise, and Virginia Maksymowicz. "Judy Chicago Birthing Art." *Witness* 74, no. 12, 12 December 1991.

"'Worthy Causes' in Tsena-Rena" compiled by Naomi Danis. *Lilith* (Spring 1991): 32.

1990

Ballatore, Sandy. "Judy Chicago's Fibre Art." *Fibrearts* (Summer 1990).

Barras, Jonetta Rose. "UDC Facing Growing Debt, Status Review." *Washington Times*, 25 July 1990.

Barras, Jonetta Rose. "Financial Inquiries Crash *The Dinner Party* at UDC." *Washington Times*, 20 July 1990.

Barras, Jonetta Rose. "D.C. Council's 'Sanity' Questioned as Hill Learns of *The Dinner Party*." *Washington Times*, 19 July 1990.

Barras, Jonetta Rose. "UDC's $1.6 Million 'Dinner'." *Washington Times*, 18 July 1990.

Berenbaum, Michael. "The Mystifying Burden of Goodness." *Dimensions: A Journal of Holocaust Studies* (1990): 21.

Bird, Kay. "House Action Smacks of Anti-Feminism-Artist." *Santa Fe New Mexican*, 6 August 1990.

"D.C. Under the Thumb Again." *Washington Post*, 31 July 1990: editorial.

"*The Dinner Party*." *Albuquerque Journal*, 17 September 1990: editorial.

Faust, Wolfgang Max. "Aufstand gegen den guten Geschmack (An Uprising Against Good Taste)." *Art Magazine* (September 1990): 44.

Gamarekian, Barbara. "A Feminist Artwork for University Library." *New York Times*, 21 July 1990.

Harrison, Keith. "UDC Trustee Wants Artwork Reconsidered." *Washington Post*, 30 July 1990.

Hickox, Katie. "Work by Santa Fe Artist Stirs Congressional Fray." *Santa Fe New Mexican*, 28 July 1996, sec. A:1.

Jackson, Susan. "Investigating How 'The Other Half' Creates." *Japan Times*, 27 May 1990.

Long, Nira Hardon. "*The Dinner Party*." *Arts Advocate* (September–October 1990).

Long, Nira Hardon. "*The Dinner Party*: A Matter of Basic Human Liberties." *Washington Post*, 9 August 1990.

Mahler, Richard. "The Battle of Chicago." *Los Angeles Times*, 12 October 1990, sec. F:1, 24.

Mann, Judy. "Art and Sexual Power." *Washington Post*, 12 September 1990.

Richardson, Congressman Bill. "Not a Vote on Art." *Santa Fe New Mexican*, 16 August 1990.

Sinclair, Molly. "An Artist's Open-Ended Invitation." *Washington Post*, 21 July 1990.

Statesline. *USA Today*, 20 July 1990.

Strand, John. "Washington D.C.: '3-D Pornography!'." *Art International Winter* (1990): 26.

Suh, Mary. "Guess Who's Not Coming to Dinner." *Ms.* (September–October 1990).

Sweets, Ellen. "The Chicago Story." *Dallas Morning News*, 16 September 1990.

"U. of the District of Columbia's Decision to Acquire Controversial Artwork Angers Some on Campus." *Chronicle of Higher Learning*, 1 August 1990.

"UDC's 'Dinner Party'." *Washington Post*, 24 July 1990.

"Washington, D.C.: University Won't Host *The Dinner Party*." *ARTnews* (December 1990): 61–62.

1989

"American Women Artists, the 20th Century." Catalog for Knoxville Museum of Art (1989).

"Fear of Others: Art Against Racism." Catalog for Arts in Action Society, Vancouver, British Columbia, Canada (September 1989).

Kubitza, Anna. "The Pink Sneakers (Die Rasafarbenen Turnschuhe)." *Lichtblick-Feminisische Kunstzeitschrift* (Fall 1989): 8–11.

1988

Aptheker, Bettina. "Standing on Our Own Ground." *Gallerie* 1, no. 1 (Annual 1988).

Bell, June D. "Setting the Table for Changes, an Artist Discusses Her Work." *Melbourne Times Leader*, 3 November 1988.

"Committed to Print." Catalog for The Museum of Modern Art, New York (1988), 57, 103.

Gray, Sharon. "Weep, Be Moved and Drink Wine." *Melbourne Age*, 30 January 1988.

Pisano, Ronald. "One Hundred Years: A Centennial Celebration of the National Association of Women Artists." Catalog for Nassau County (New York) Museum of Fine Art (1988): 4, 38.

"Table for 39 Looks for a Home, A." *Melbourne Times on Sunday*, 17 January 1988.

1987

"*Art & The Law*." Catalog, West Publishing, 1987, 1984.

Kuperstein, Elana. "Judy Chicago: A Feminist Artist in Search of Her Jewish Self." *B'nai B'rith Women's World* 78, no. 3 (April 1987).

Netsky, Ron. "Judy Chicago's Style of Creation." *Democrat and Chronicle,* 14 January 1987.

Roessner, Barbara T. "Bearing Children Is What Women Do." *International Herald Tribune,* 13 March 1987.

1986

"*American Art/American Women 1965–1985.*" Catalog for Stamford Museum, Stamford, CT (1986).

Chamaj, Betty. "Visions and Revisions: Women's Studies and the Challenge to See Anew." *Frontiers: A Journal of Women's Studies* 8, no. 3 (1986).

Lippard, Lucy. "*Por Encima Del Bloqueo.*" Catalog for Ministerio de Cultura de Cuba (1986).

Thompson, Ruthie. "Judy Chicago's *Birth Project.*" *Screen Printing* (1986).

1985

Battiata, Mary. "Judy Chicago's Tapestry of Birth." *Washington Post,* 13 May 1985.

Bennetts, Leslie. "Judy Chicago: Women's Lives and Art." *New York Times,* 8 April 1985.

Harper, Paula. "*Powerplay.*" Catalog for exhibition at ACA Galleries, New York (1985).

Januszczak, Waldemer. "Look Who's Coming to Dinner." *Guardian Women* (London) 19 March 1985.

Lauter, Estella. "Acts of Creation." *Women's Review of Books* 2, no. 12 (September 1985).

Lippard, Lucy. "Born Again." *Village Voice,* 16 April 1985.

McWilliams, Martha. "Judy Chicago Strikes Again: The *Birth Project.*" *Washington Review* (October–November 1985).

Stein, Judith. "Midwife to the Revolution." *New York Times Book Review,* 15 September 1985.

1984

Butterfield, Jan. "Judy Chicago 1973–1983." Catalog for exhibition at ACA Galleries, New York (May 1984).

1983

Blair, Gwenda. "Reviewing the *Birth Project*-Judy Chicago's Judgement Day." *Village Voice,* 1 November 1983.

"Interview with Judy Chicago by Arlene Raven and Susan Rennie." *Chrysalis,* no. 4 (1983).

Keerdoja, Eileen. "Judy Chicago's Controversial Creation." *Newsweek,* 31 October 1983.

Roth, Moira. "The Amazing Decade: Women and Performance Art in America." *Astro Artz,* 1983.

1982

Blair, Gwenda. "The Womanly Art of Judy Chicago." *Mademoiselle* (January 1982).

Cox, Meg. "Making Art with a Female Message." *Wall Street Journal,* 8 January 1982.

Freeman, Natalie V. "A Dream of a Dinner Party–Judy Chicago." *City Woman* (Spring 1982).

Freeman, Natalie V. "Revelations of a Private Female World." *Macleans,* 5 April 1982.

Mays, John Bently. "Epic Dinner Party Strikes to the Core." *Toronto Globe and Mail,* May 1982.

1981

Adams, Jane. "Judy Chicago." *Horizon* (March 1981).

Berger, Suzanne. "Dinner Party Comes to Chicago." *Sister Source,* 1 August 1981, 1–7.

Evett, David. "Moveable Feast." *Northern Ohio Live,* 4–17 May 1981, 27–29.

Mullarkey, Maureen. "Dishing It Out: Judy Chicago's *Dinner Party.*" *Commonweal* 108, no. 7 (April 1981): 210–211.

Seebohm, C. "*The Dinner Party*: Turning Women's Crafts into Art." *House & Garden* (April 1981).

"*Southern Cal Artists 1940–80.*" Catalog from Laguna Beach Museum of Art, California (1981).

Wachtel, Eleanor. "This Is Judy Chicago." *Homemaker's Magazine* (November 1981): 34.

1980

"Chicago's *Dinner Party* Comes to Brooklyn Museum." *New York Times,* 17 October 1980, sec. C:1.

Hughes, Robert. "An Obsessive Feminist Pantheon: Judy Chicago's *Dinner Party* Turns History into Agitprop." *Time,* 15 December 1980, 85.

Lippard, Lucy. "Judy Chicago's *Dinner Party.*" *Art in America* (April 1980): 115–126.

Mitgang, Herbert. "Publishing: Judy Chicago Speaking in Volumes." *New York Times,* 26 September 1980.

Perrault, John. "No Reservations." *Soho News,* 22 October 1980, 1.

Tennant, Donna. "'Right Out of History' a Remarkable Story." *Houston Chronicle,* 14 March 1980.

Wolfert, Lee. "Sassy Judy Chicago Throws *A Dinner Party,* but the Art World Mostly Sends Regrets." *People,* 8 December 1980, 156.

1979

Albright, Thomas. "Guess Who's Coming to Dinner." *ARTnews,* January 1979.

Berger, Arthur. "Nourishing Art from the Rich History of Women." *Chronicle of Higher Education,* 16 April 1979.

Butterfield, Jan. "Guess Who's Coming to Judy Chicago's Dinner." *Mother Jones* (January 1979): 23.

"Feminist Sculptor's *Dinner Party,* A." *New York Times,* 1 April 1979.

Fischer, Hal. "Judy Chicago, San Francisco Museum of Art." *Artforum* (Summer 1979): 77.

Glueck, Grace. "Judy Chicago's Rochester *Dinner Party* Is Canceled." *New York Times,* 11 August 1979.

Hamilton, Mildred. "The Dinner Party." *Graduate Woman* (July–August 1979).

"Judy Chicago's *The Dinner Party,* Two Views of the First Feminist Epic Artwork." *Village Voice,* 11 June 1979.

Kingsley, April. "The I-Hate-to-Cook *Dinner Party.*" *Ms.* (June 1979).

Larson, Kay. "Under the Table: Duplicity, Alienation." *Village Voice,* 11 June 1979, 51.

Lipinski, Ann Marie. "Judy Chicago's *Dinner Party.*" *Chicago Tribune,* 19 August 1979.

Lippard, Lucy. "*Dinner Party* a Four-Star Treat." *Seven Days* (April 1979).

Muchnic, Suzanne. "An Intellectual Famine at Judy Chicago's Feast." *Los Angeles Times,* 15 April 1979.

Roth, Moira. "Connecting Conversations." *Smith Publications* (1979).

Stevens, Mark. "Guess Who's Coming to Dinner." *Newsweek*, 2 April 1979, 93.

"Table for 39, A." *Life* (May 1979).

Woo, Elaine. "Judy Chicago's *The Dinner Party*." *Los Angeles Herald Examiner*, 20 March 1979.

Zolotow, Maurice. "The 78 Most Interesting People in Los Angeles." *Los Angeles* (November 1979): 203.

1978

Isenberg, Barbara. "Invitation to a *Dinner Party*." *Los Angeles Times*, 6 April 1978.

"Judy Chicago: World of the China Painter." *Ceramics Monthly* (May 1978): 40–45.

1977

Hass, Charlie. "Judy Chicago's *Dinner Party*: A Room of Her Own." *New West*, 1 August 1977.

Heresies: A Feminist Publication on Art and Politics 1 (1977): 107.

"Judy Chicago: China Painter" *Ceramics Monthly* (June 1977): 34–35.

"*Overglaze Imagery: Cone 019–016.*" Catalog for Visual Arts Center, California State University Fullerton (1977).

"Painting and Sculpture in California: The Modern Era." Catalog for San Francisco Museum of Modern Art (1977): 161, 165, 205.

Raven, Arlene, and Susan Rennie. "*The Dinner Party* Project: An Interview with Judy Chicago." *Chrysalis*, no. 4 (1977): 96.

Wilding, Faith. "By Our Own Hands." *Double X* (1977).

1976

"*American Artist's '76: A Celebration.*" Catalog for the Marion Koogler McNay Art Institute (1976).

Butterfield, Jan. "Interview with Judy Chicago." *City of San Francisco* (January 1976).

1974

Chicago, Judy, and Arlene Raven. "Letter to a Young Woman Artist." *Anonymous Was a Woman*, California Institute of the Arts, 1974, 67–68.

Lippard, Lucy. "Judy Chicago Talking to Lucy R. Lippard." *Artforum* (September 1974).

1973

Chicago, Judy, and Miriam Schapiro. "Female Imagery." *Womanspace Journal* 1, no. 3 (Summer 1973).

Chicago, Judy, and Arlene Raven. "An Evening with Judy Chicago." Pacifica Radio Archives, Los Angeles, 9 January 1973.

Chicago, Judy, and Arlene Raven. "Women's Art History." Pacifica Radio Archives, Los Angeles, 2 January 1973.

1972

Chicago, Judy, and Miriam Schapiro. Statement in *Womanhouse*. Catalog on the collaborative project created by the Feminist Art Program, California Institute of the Arts, and Introduction (1972).

Chicago, Judy, and Dextra Frankel. Introduction to *Invisible/Visible*. Catalog for Long Beach Museum of Art (April 1972).

1971

Chicago, Judy. Statement in "Miss Chicago and the California Girls." *Everywoman II*, no. 7, 7 May 1971.

1970

Chicago, Judy. Advertisement announcing name change from Judy Gerowitz to Judy Chicago. *Artforum* (October 1970): 20.

1969

Chicago, Judy. "Notes" as a catalog for *Judy Gerowitz*, One-Woman Show at the Pasadena Art Museum, 28 April to 1 June 1969.

1968

"*The West Coast Now—Current Work from the Western Seaboard.*" Catalog for Portland Art Museum (1968).

SELECTED FILMOGRAPHY

The Dinner Party: Art for Our Sake. Featuring Lily Tomlin. Filmmakers Kate Amend and Johanna Demetrakas. 15 minutes. Through the Flower Corporation, 1995. Videocassette.

A Family of Women. Produced by Vu Productions. Aired June 1994 on Turner Broadcasting.

"*From Darkness into Light,*" *the Making of the Holocaust Project*. Filmmaker Kate Amend. 29 minutes. 1994. Videocassette.

Holocaust Project: Judy Chicago. Produced by Viking/Penguin. Aired: Tampa, on WFLA/NBC; Miami, on WPLG/ABC; Detroit, on WJBK/CBS, 28 October 1993; Fairfield, on Connecticut Cable/Noon News, 19 October 1993; Minneapolis, on WCCO/CBS, 25 November 1993; Sacramento, on KOVR/ABC, 5 November 1993; Albuquerque, on KRQE/CBS, 19 October 1993; San Francisco, on KGO/ABC; Nashville, on WTVF/CBS, 19 October 1993; National, on ABC News One, 19 October 1993; Richmond, on WWBT/NBC, 22 October 1993; Atlanta, on WAGA/NBC, 20 October 1993; National, on Conus Communications, 16 November 1993.

Holocaust Project. Filmmaker Matthew Sneddon. Produced by "Colores," KNME, Albuquerque, NM, 1993.

Judy Chicago and the California Girls. Produced by Judith Dankoff. 1970.

"Century of Women: Part 3." Judy Chicago and The Dinner Party featured in TBS film and accompanying book, broadcast on TBS, 9 June 1994.

Judy Chicago: The Birth Project. Filmmaker Vivian Kleiman. 20 minutes. Vivian Kleiman Productions, 1985. Videocassette.

Right Out of History: The Making of Judy Chicago's Dinner Party. Filmmaker Johanna Demetrakas. 60 minutes. Phoenix Films, 1980. Videocassette.

Under Wraps. Produced by Starry Night Production, Inc. 56 minutes. 1996. Videocassette.

Womanhouse. Filmmaker Johanna Demetrakas. 47 minutes. Phoenix Films, 1974. Videocassette.

World's Most Intriguing Women on E! Produced by Francine Weinberg. E!
    Entertainment Television, 1997.
Judy Chicago and the California Girls. Produced by Judith Dankoff. 1970.

THESES AND DISSERTATIONS

Bickell, Rosalind. "Intervention on the Sacred: The Politics and Poetics of *The
    Dinner Party.*" Paper, 1991.
Duncan, Sally Anne. "Judy Chicago's *Holocaust Project*: Contexts and Connections."
    Presented at the symposium "Locating Feminism at Brown University in 1996."
Edwards, Janis. "Rhetoric in the Visual Image: Judy Chicago's *The Dinner Party.*"
    Thesis for Master of Arts in Communication Studies at California State
    University, Sacramento, CA, Fall 1985.
Jensen, Lisa H. "Responses to a Feminist Perspective in Art: Judy Chicago's *Dinner
    Party* and the Language of its Critics." Unpublished paper from Judy Chicago
    archives, 1980.
Kubitza, Anette. "Judy Chicago's *The Dinner Party* Im Kontext Feministischer
    Diskurse." Wissenschaftliche Hausarbeit zur Erlangung des akademischen
    Grades eines Magister Artium der Universitat Hamburg, Hamburg, Germany,
    1991.
Meyer, Laura. "The 'Essential' Judy Chicago: Central Core Imagery vs. The
    Language of Fetishism in *Womanhouse* and *The Dinner Party.*" Thesis for
    Master of Arts at University of California at Riverside, 1994.
Padawar, Nadine. "Till Death Do Us Part?: The Sexual Objectification of Women in
    Art and Advertising." Senior Thesis in Women's Studies, 1991.
Popp, Christine M. "What's In An Image?: Judy Chicago's *The Dinner Party.*"
    Honor's Thesis, 1991.
Thompson Wylder, Viki. "Judy Chicago's *Dinner Party* and *Birth Project* as Religious
    Symbol and Visual Theology." Dissertation for Doctor of Philosophy at Florida
    State University, Tallahassee, FL, Spring 1993.

MANUSCRIPT COLLECTIONS

Selected papers of Judy Chicago donated to the Schlesinger Library at Radcliffe
    College, Cambridge, MA, 1997.

CATALOG

Page 5 *Childhood Fingerpainting*, 1943, (Age 4), fingerpaint on paper, 14 1/2 x 18 1/2 inches. Collection: Elizabeth A. Sackler. Page 8 *Drawing*, 1950, (Age 11), mixed media on colored paper, 18 x 24 inches. Page 9 *Self-portrait: Self-loathing*, 1959, (Age 20), graphite on newsprint, 24 x 18 inches. Page 23 *Car Hood*, 1964, sprayed acrylic lacquer on car hood, 48 x 72 inches. Collection: Elaine and Rad Sutnar. Photo: Through the Flower Archives. Page 24 *Mother Superette*, 1964, acrylic on paper, 19 x 26 inches. Collection: Elizabeth A. Sackler. Page 25 *Trinity*, 1965, canvas, plywood, and sprayed lacquer, base: 60 x 128 x 63 inches (installed). Collection: The Artist, courtesy of Flanders Contemporary Art, Minneapolis, MN. *Aluminum Game Board*, 1965, sandblasted aluminum, 7 x 18 x 18 inches. Collection: Elyse and Stanley Grinstein. *Bronze Domes*, 1968, formed acrylic inside successive formed clear acrylic domes with sprayed acrylic lacquer, base: 38 1/2 x 30 x 30 inches. Collection: The Artist, courtesy of Flanders Contemporary Art, Minneapolis, MN. Page 26 *Pasadena Lifesavers– Red Series #4*, 1969–1970, sprayed acrylic lacquer on acrylic, 60 x 60 inches. Collection: Mary Ross Taylor. Photo: Through the Flower Archives. Page 27 *Sky Flesh*, from the *Fleshgarden* series, 1971, sprayed acrylic lacquer on acrylic, 96 x 96 inches. Collection: Elizabeth A. Sackler. Page 29 *Silver Doorways* (Proof E), 1972, lithograph and hand-colored collage, 22 x 22 inches. Collection: Elizabeth A. Sackler. Page 30 *Christina of Sweden*, from the *Great Ladies* series, 1972, sprayed acrylic on canvas, 40 x 40 inches. Collection: Elizabeth A. Sackler. Page 31 *Elizabeth, in Honor of Elizabeth*, from the *Great Ladies* series, 1973, sprayed acrylic on canvas, 40 x 40 inches. Collection: Elizabeth A. Sackler. Page 32 *Marie Antoinette*, from the *Great Ladies* series, 1973, sprayed acrylic on canvas, 40 x 40 inches. Collection: Elizabeth A. Sackler. Page 33 *Transformation Drawing–Great Ladies Changing into Butterflies*, 1973, Prismacolor on paper, 23 x 23 inches. Collection: Elizabeth A. Sackler. Page 34 *Through the Flower (Into the Darkness)*, 1973, Prismacolor on rag, 5 x 5 inches (image), 11 x 11 inches (mounting). Collection: Elizabeth A. Sackler. Page 35 *Through the Flower*, 1973, sprayed acrylic on canvas, 60 x 60 inches. Collection: Elizabeth A. Sackler. Page 36 *Let It All Hang Out*, 1973, sprayed acrylic on canvas, 80 x 80 inches. Collection: New Orleans Museum of Art. Photo: Courtesy of New Orleans Museum of Art, 2001. Page 37 *Heaven Is for White Men Only*, 1973, sprayed acrylic on canvas, 80 x 80 inches. Collection: New Orleans Museum of Art. Photo: Courtesy of New Orleans Museum of Art, 2001. Page 38 *Female Rejection Drawing #1 (How Does It Feel to Be Rejected?)*, from *Rejection Quintet*, 1974, Prismacolor on rag, 29 x 23 inches. Collection: San Francisco Museum of Modern Art. Photo: Through the Flower Archives. Page 39 *Female Rejection Drawing #2 (Childhood Rejection)*, from *Rejection Quintet*, 1974, Prismacolor on rag, 29 x 23 inches. Collection: San Francisco Museum of Modern Art. Photo: Through the Flower Archives. Page 40 *Female Rejection Drawing #3 (Peeling Back)*, from *Rejection Quintet*, 1974, Prismacolor on rag, 29 x 23 inches. Collection: San Francisco Museum of Modern Art. Photo: Through the Flower Archives. *Female Rejection Drawing #4 (Rejection Fantasy)*, from *Rejection Quintet*, 1974, Prismacolor on rag, 29 x 23 inches. Collection: San Francisco Museum of Modern Art. Photo: Through the Flower Archives. Page 41 *Female Rejection Drawing #5 (How Does It Feel to Expose Your Real Identity?)*, from *Rejection Quintet*, 1974, Prismacolor on rag, 29 x 23 inches. Collection: San Francisco Museum of Modern Art. Photo: Through the Flower Archives. Page 42 *Butterfly Vagina Erotica*, 1975, lithographs, cover page: 11 1/4 x 21 3/4 inches, each page: 10 x 10 inches. Page 43 *Did You Know Your Mother Had a Sacred Heart?*, 1976, china paint and pen work on porcelain, embroidery on silk, and teak wood, 54 x 110 inches. Collection: Los Angeles County Museum of Art, Gift of Mary Ross Taylor. Photo: 2001 Museum Associates/Los Angeles County Museum of Art. Page 45 *The Dinner Party*, installation view, 1979, 36 x 516 x 576 inches. Collection: Brooklyn Museum of Art, Gift of The Elizabeth A. Sackler Foundation. Pages 46–47 *Butterfly*, test plates, 1973–1974, china paint on porcelain, each 12 1/2 inches in diameter. Judy Chicago in the china painting studio, circa 1974. Photo: Through the Flower Archives. Pages 48–49 *The Dinner Party* banners, 1979, modified

Aubusson tapestry, each banner: 60 x 36 inches [6 banners]. Installation for *The Dinner Party* banners, 1996, UCLA Armand Hammer Museum, Los Angeles, CA. Page 50 *Hypatia*, study for runner back, 1979, gouache and ink on paper, 18 1/2 x 35 1/4 inches. Page 51 *Hypatia*, study for illuminated letter, 1977, Prismacolor on paper, 12 1/4 x 16 1/2 inches. Page 52 *Hypatia*, test plate, 1979, china paint on porcelain, 14 inches in diameter. Page 53 *The Dinner Party* (detail), 1979, Hypatia place setting, mixed media. Page 54 *Eleanor of Aquitaine*, test plate, 1979, china paint on porcelain, 14 inches in diameter. Collection: Audrey and Bob Cowan. Page 55 *Eleanor of Aquitaine*, gridded runner drawing, 1979, ink on vellum, 56 x 30 inches. Page 56 *Eleanor of Aquitaine*, study for runner, 1977, Prismacolor and graphite on rag paper, 29 x 23 inches. Collection: Audrey and Bob Cowan. Page 57 *The Dinner Party* (detail), 1979, Eleanor of Aquitaine place setting, mixed media. Page 58 *Petronilla de Meath*, plate drawing, 1976, Prismacolor on rag, 18 1/2 x 21 1/2 inches. *Petronilla de Meath*, test plate, 1979, china paint on porcelain, 14 inches in diameter. *Petronilla de Meath*, study for illuminated letter, 1977, Prismacolor on rag, 15 x 22 inches (framed). Page 59 *The Dinner Party* (detail), 1979, Petronilla de Meath place setting, mixed media. Page 60 *Mary Wollstonecraft*, test plate, 1979, bisque porcelain, 14 inches in diameter. *Mary Wollstonecraft*, gridded runner drawing, 1979, ink on vellum, 56 x 30 inches. Page 61 *The Dinner Party* (detail), 1979, Mary Wollstonecraft place setting, mixed media. Page 62 *Emily Dickinson*, study for plate, 1977, ink, photo, and collage on rag paper, 22 1/2 x 34 1/2 inches. Collection: The National Museum of Women in the Arts. Page 63 *The Dinner Party* (detail), 1979, Emily Dickinson place setting, mixed media. Page 64 *Margaret Sanger*, test plate, 1979, china paint on porcelain, 14 inches in diameter. Collection: Dorothy and Junie Sinson. *Margaret Sanger*, gridded runner drawing, 1979, ink on vellum, 56 x 30 inches. Page 65 *The Dinner Party* (detail), 1979, Margaret Sanger place setting, mixed media. Page 66 *Virginia Woolf*, test plate, 1978, glazed porcelain, 14 inches in diameter. Collection: Elizabeth A. Sackler. *Virginia Woolf*, study, 1978, mixed media drawing, 24 x 36 inches. Collection: Mary Ross Taylor. Page 67 *The Dinner Party* (detail), 1979, Virginia Woolf place setting and runner, mixed media. Page 69 *The Crowning*, 1981, Prismacolor on black Arches, 30 x 40 inches. Collection: Private. Pages 70-71 *In the Beginning*, 1982, Prismacolor on Black Canson, 61 x 367 inches. Page 72 *Birth* drawing, 1981, Prismacolor on fabric, 18 x 31 inches. Page 73 *Birth Tear*, 1982, embroidery on silk, 20 1/2 x 27 1/2 inches. Needlework by Jane Thompson. Collection: Albuquerque Museum of Art. Page 74 *Birth Trinity*, 1983, needlework on six-mesh canvas, 51 x 130 inches. Needlework by the Teaneck, NJ Group. Collection: Albuquerque Museum of Art. Photo: Through the Flower Archives. Page 75 *The Creation*, 1984, modified Aubusson tapestry, 43 x 163 inches. Collection: Audrey and Bob Cowan. Page 76 Drawing for *Smocked Figure*, 1984, Prismacolor and graphite on rag, 24 x 20 inches. Collection: Albuquerque Museum of Art. Installation for *Smocked Figure*, 1984, each panel: 14 x 11 inches [5 panels]. Collection: Albuquerque Museum of Art. Page 77 *Smocked Figure*, 1984, smocking and embroidery, 62 x 22 inches (framed). Needlework by Mary Ewanoski. Collection: Albuquerque Museum of Art. Page 79 *Woe/Man*, 1986, multipatinated bronze, 48 x 36 x 5 inches. Collection: Elizabeth A. Sackler. Page 80 *Come Here/Go Away*, 1984, Conté crayon on Arches, 30 x 22 inches. Page 81 Study 2 for *In the Shadow of the Handgun*, 1983, acrylic and Prismacolor on rag paper, 22 x 30 inches. Pages 82-83 *Three Faces of Man*, 1985, sprayed acrylic and oil on Belgian linen, triptych, each panel: 54 x 36 inches [3 panels]. Collection: Ruth Lambert and Henry S. Harrison. Page 84 *Really Sad/Power Mad*, 1986, Prismacolor and pastel on rag paper, 27 x 39 inches. Study for *Doublehead I*, 1986, Prismacolor and ink on hand-made paper, 29 x 21 inches. Page 85 *Lavender Doublehead/Hold Me*, 1986, sprayed acrylic and oil on hand-cast paper, 51 x 39 1/2 x 3 inches. Pages 86-87 *Driving the World to Destruction*, 1985, sprayed acrylic and oil on Belgian linen, 108 x 168 inches. Page 89 *Holocaust Project Logo*, 1984, stained glass, 47 x 54 inches. Pages 90-91 *The Fall*, 1993, modified Aubusson tapestry, 68 3/4 x 225 inches. Woven by Audrey Cowan. Collection: Judy Chicago and Audrey Cowan. Page 92 *Vetruvian Man, The Measure?*, 1987, Prismacolor, ink, gouache, and micrography on Arches, 32 1/2 x 44 1/4 inches. Page 93 *Stairway to Death*, 1989, Prismacolor and ink washes on paper, 25 x 33 inches. Pages 94-95 *What Would You Have Done?*, Judy Chicago with photography by Donald Woodman, 1989, sprayed acrylic, photo oil and photography, 26 x 58 inches. Page 96 *Soul Murder*, study for *Im/Balance of Power*, Judy Chicago with photography by Donald Woodman, 1991, mixed media and photography on photo linen and rag paper, diptych, each painting: 23 x 29 inches.

Page 97 *Im/Balance of Power*, Judy Chicago with photography by Donald Woodman, 1989, sprayed acrylic, oil, and photography on photo linen, 77 x 95 inches. Collection: The Artists and Through the Flower. Pages 98-99 *Pink Triangle/Torture*, Judy Chicago with photography by Donald Woodman, 1988, photography and Prismacolor on paper, 46 x 53 inches. Page 100 *Pansy Crucifixion*, Judy Chicago with photography by Donald Woodman, 1988, colored photographs, Prismacolor, acrylic wash and ink on rag, 32 x 30 inches. Page 101 Final study for *Lesbian Triangle*, Judy Chicago with photography by Donald Woodman, 1989, sprayed acrylic, oil, Prismacolor, and photography on photo linen and rag paper, 53 x 46 inches (framed). Collection: Elizabeth A. Sackler. Pages 102-103 *Arbeit Macht Frei/Work Makes Who Free?*, 1992, sprayed acrylic, oil, welded metal, wood, and photography on photo linen and canvas, 67 x 143 inches. Collection: The Artists and Through the Flower Corporation. Page 104-105 *Four Questions*, (view from left, frontal view, view from right), Judy Chicago with photography by Donald Woodman, 1993, sprayed acrylic, Marshall photo oils, Prismacolor on Polaroid transfer on paper mounted on wood, 17 x 53 inches. Collection: The Artists and Through the Flower Corporation. Pages 106-107 *Rainbow Shabbat*, 1992, 54 x 192 inches (installed), stained glass. Collection: The Artists and Through the Flower Corporation. Page 109 *Find It in Your Heart*, 2000, carved wood, embroidery, Japanese gold embroidery and cording, 78 x 50 x 38 inches. Needlework by Paula Daves and Lynda Patterson. Collection: Judy Chicago, Paula Daves, and Lynda Patterson. Pages 110-111 *My dove in the clefts of the rock, O For your scent, How fine you are, my love, Yes, I am black and radiant, There you stand like a palm*, and *Come, let us go out to the open fields*. All six pieces from *Voices from the Song of Songs*, 1998-2000, lithograph/heliorelief/ hand-coloring on Shiramine Japanese paper, twelve prints, each: 24 x 20 inches. Courtesy Graphic Studio. Page 112 *Arcanum in Shades of Gray*, 2000, chromatic erosion and acrylic paint on four laminated glass panels, each panel: 29 x 19, base: 36 x 32 x 50 inches. *Peeling Back (after* Female Rejection Drawing #3*) 2000*, chromatic erosion and paint on laminated glass, 24 13/16 x 24 11/16 inches. Pages 113-115 *Autobiography of a Year: June 1993 to November 1994 I & II*, mixed media unbound artist's book on paper in two boxed sets, 140 drawings, each drawing: 15 x 11 inches or 11 x 15 inches, installed: 60 x 84 inches.

INDEX